Making Sense of Phrasal Verbs

Martin Shovel

ENGLISH LANGUAGE TEACHING

Prentice Hall

New York London Toronto Sydney Tokyo Singapore

To Martha

Published 1992 by
Prentice Hall International (UK) Limited
Campus 400, Maylands Avenue
Hemel Hempstead, Herts HP2 7EZ
a division of
Simon & Schuster International Group

First published 1985 by Cassell Publishers Limited.

Printed and bound in Great Britain by The Bath Press, Avon.
Designed by Janet McCallum
Phototypset by Chapterhouse, The Cloisters, Formby

British Library Cataloguing in Publication Data

Information available from the publisher on request.

ISBN 0-13-554833-0

1 2 3 4 5 96 95 94 93 92

Contents

Introduction

Making Sense of Phrasal Verbs presents a selection of the most useful and frequently used phrasal verbs in the English language. It avoids the use of grammatical classifications because such classifications are often more complicated and difficult than the phrasal verbs they are used to teach. Instead, the aim is to increase the learner's confidence by presenting phrasal verbs in a lively and straightforward way using illustrations and question-prompts.

Making Sense of Phrasal Verbs can be used for self-study, for pairwork, for conventional class or group teaching, and as a reference book. It is intended for intermediate students of English as a second or foreign language. Students studying for the First Certificate Examination will find the book especially useful.

The book contains twenty units, each of which introduces and practises six separate phrasal verbs. At the back of the book there is a reference section in which the phrasal verbs are listed in alphabetical order.

Illustrations and question-prompts
Each phrasal verb is introduced using illustrations and question-prompts. The question-prompts are designed to focus the learner's attention and help him or her make an informed guess at the meaning of the phrasal verb. The guess is expected to take the form of a paraphrase or synonym. The learner is *not* expected to produce a dictionary-type definition.

Reference section
The reference section contains an alphabetical listing of all the phrasal verbs presented in the book. Each entry includes:
- a list of words and phrases that can be used with the phrasal verb
- a clear definition
- a context sentence or sentences related to the introductory illustrations
- easy to read structural information showing the positioning of noun phrases and pronouns

Practice section
Each unit has a practice section consisting of a variety of exercises. The exercises are very controlled to begin with and then gradually lead to free-production. All six phrasal verbs in the unit should be studied first before the practice section is done.

A NOTE ON PHRASAL VERBS

A phrasal verb is a compound verb formed by one of the following combinations: (1) verb and adverb; or (2) verb and preposition; or (3) verb with both adverb and preposition. Phrasal verbs are an essential part of the English language – especially the spoken language. Simple combinations like *sit down* and *stand up* cause the learner few problems. The difficulties begin when the combination is 'idiomatic': that is, when the meaning of the combination as a whole (i.e. the phrasal verb) is different from the meanings of its separate parts. The learner may, for example, know the meaning of the verb *break* and the meaning of the adverb *down*, but this knowledge will not help him or her to understand the different meanings of the phrasal verb *break down*. All the phrasal verbs in this book are idiomatic, and each different meaning is treated as a separate phrasal verb.

Unit 1

Where is the man?
What do you think he wants to do?
Do you think he knows which platform to go to?

Who is he talking to?
Before he can catch his train he has to do something.
Make a sentence describing what he is doing.
Think of another way of saying **find out**.
Now turn to page 89 to check your answer.

look for

Where is the man's right hand?
Why?
What is he thinking about?

Where is the man's hand now?
Has he got a key?
Can he find it?
Make a sentence describing what he is doing.
Think of another way of saying **look for**.
Now turn to page 92 to check your answer.

look up

What is the man doing?
Do you think he understands what he is reading?

What is he reading now?
Why?
In the first picture the man found a word he couldn't understand.
Make a sentence describing what he is doing to find the meaning of the word.
Think of another way of saying **look up**.
Now turn to page 92 to check your answers.

look over

Where is the man?
Why do you think he is there?
Do you think he wants to buy the car?
What is he doing?
Why?

What is he doing now?
Why?
If the car is in good condition what is the man going to do?
Make a sentence describing what he is doing to check the condition of the car.
Think of another way of saying **look over**.
Now turn to page 92 to check your answer.

Unit 1

look round

Look at the two people on the left.
Do you think they are married?
Do you think it is their house?
What is the man on the right doing?
What's his job?

Are they inside the house?
What are they going to do if they like the house?
Make a sentence describing what they are doing.
Think of another way of saying **look round**.
Now turn to page 92 to check your answer.

look into

What has happened to the man on the ground?
Is he dead?
Who are the men in uniform?
Do they know what happened to the dead man?
Do the police want more information about what has happened?
Make a sentence describing what the police are doing.
Think of another way of saying **look into**.
Now turn to page 92 to check your answer.

Complete these sentences using the six verbs from this unit. Use each verb only once.

1 This gentleman thinks the service in our hotel is terrible. We must _____ his complaint immediately.
2 Where is the cat? I've been _____ it all day.
3 We can _____ where he lives by looking at the map.
4 I want to know the time of the London train so I'll _____ it _____ in the timetable.
5 I'd like a few days to _____ the report before I make a decision.
6 When we were in London we spent a few hours _____ the British Museum.

Complete these sentences with verbs from this unit. Each sentence has more than one possible answer. Give all possible answers.

1 Pass me the address book and I'll _____ the number of his house.
2 Let's _____ the house once more before we decide to buy it.

Replace the words in italics by the words in brackets. Change the word order if necessary.
EXAMPLE Bill found *it* out. (the number)
         Bill found out the number.

1 Jane looked up *the date*. (it)
2 We looked for *the dog*. (it)
3 I'd like to look *it* over. (the report)
4 Let's look round *it*. (the city)
5 We found out *the truth*. (it)
6 We are looking into *it*. (the situation)

Complete the passage using **find out/look into/look for.**

The police are _____ yesterday's bank robbery. They are trying to _____ how the robbers managed to open the safe. At the moment detectives are _____ four men who escaped in a black getaway car.

Complete the passage using **look up/look over/look round.**

The other day I was _____ an antique shop when I found an old encyclopedia. I _____ it _____ and decided to buy it. When I got home I opened it and _____ the capital of China.

Use the verbs in brackets to reply to the following.
EXAMPLE I don't know how to spell that word. (look up)
POSSIBLE REPLY Why don't you **look** it **up** in your dictionary.

1 The salesmen in your store are very rude. What are you going to do about my complaint? (look into)
2 How can I get John's telephone number? (look up)
3 What are you doing under the table? (look for)
4 Will you sign this document now? (look over)
5 What did you do in town today? (look round)
6 Do you know who that man is? (find out)

Unit 2

take after

Do you think these two people are related?
What do you think their relationship is?
Do you think they look alike?
Make a sentence describing the way the small boy looks compared to his father.
Think of another way of saying **take after**.

Now turn to page 95 to check your answer.

grow up

1955   1960   1985

What can you see in picture one?
How old is he in picture two?
Is he still a baby in picture three?
Make a sentence describing what is happening to him in the three pictures between 1955 and 1985.
Think of another way of saying **grow up**.

Now turn to page 91 to check your answer.

Unit 2

look after

Describe what is happening in each picture.
Make a sentence describing what the mother is doing for her baby.
Think of another way of saying **look after**.
Now turn to page 91 to check your answer.

bring up

1967   1972   1973   1985

What is the year in picture one?
What is the woman doing?
How old is her little boy in picture two?
What is his mother doing?
What is happening in pictures three and four?
Make a sentence describing what the woman did for her son between 1967 and 1985?
Think of another way of saying **bring up**.
Now turn to page 87 to check your answer.

Unit 2

do up (1)

Is this house in good condition?
How many people can you see?
What are they doing?
What do you think they are going to do?

Is the house in good condition now?
Make a sentence describing what they did to the house.
Think of another way of saying **do up**.

Now turn to page 88 to check your answer.

look back

Are the two people on the left young or old?
What do you think their relationship is?
What are they looking at?
Are they thinking about the future?
Who do you think the couple in the photograph are?
Make a sentence describing what the elderly couple are doing?
Think of another way of saying **look back**.

Now turn to page 92 to check your answer.

Complete these sentences using the six verbs from this unit. Use each verb only once.

1 My aunt _____ her family without any help from her husband.
2 Julia wants to be a teacher when she _____.
3 When I stayed in hospital the nurses _____ me very well.
4 Children often _____ their parents.
5 We must stop _____ and start thinking about the future.
6 Let's _____ the flat before we try and sell it.

Change these sentences into the passive. Do not include the agent in your answer.
EXAMPLE John's parents brought him up in the country.
         John was brought up in the country.

1 Jack's mother looked after him.
2 My parents brought me up to respect the law.
3 They did up the house before they sold it.

Replace the words in italics by the words in brackets. Change the word order if necessary.
EXAMPLE Sandra takes after *Sue*. (her)
         Sandra takes after her.

1 Aunt Jane brought up *four children*. (them)
2 Let's do *it* up. (the lounge in our new flat)
3 Mike takes after *him*. (his grandfather)
4 You should look after *them*. (your new shoes)
5 I enjoy looking back on *the old times*. (them)

Complete the passage using **grow up/bring up/look back**.

Ted was a badly-behaved child and very difficult to _____. When I _____ at his childhood it is funny to think he _____ and became a policeman.

Complete the passage using **look after/take after/do up**.

Sam _____ his father. He is very careless and doesn't _____ himself properly. Last week, for instance, he fell off a ladder while he was _____ his new house.

Use the verbs in brackets to reply to the following.
EXAMPLE Why did you buy that old car? (do up)
POSSIBLE REPLY I bought it because I'm going to **do** it **up** and sell it.

1 Your car is in very good condition. (look after)
2 This flat is in a terrible state. (do up)
3 Did you have a happy childhood? (look back)
4 He's a very polite young man. (bring up)
5 Alison is very clever. (take after)
6 Last time I saw Sally she was just a little girl. (grow up)

Unit 3

put through

What is the man doing?
Who is he speaking to?
Why do you think he is speaking to her?
Is the other telephone ringing?

Is the other telephone ringing now?
Make a sentence describing what the operator is doing to make the other telephone ring.
Think of another way of saying **put through**.
Now turn to page 94 to check your answer.

speak up

Describe the two people.
What is the young man doing?
Can the old man hear him?

Is the young man talking more quietly now?
Why not?
Can the old man hear him now?
Make a sentence describing why the old man can hear the young man now.
Think of another way of saying **speak up**.
Now turn to page 95 to check your answer.

cut off

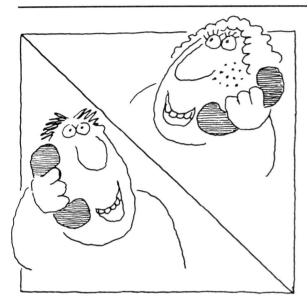

What are they doing?

Are they still talking?
Why not?
Make a sentence describing why they can't continue their conversation.
Think of another way of saying **cut off**.
Now turn to page 88 to check your answer.

hold on

What are they doing?

What is the man on the right doing?
Why do you think the other man is looking at his watch?
Make a sentence describing what the man on the left is doing while the other man is getting some information.
Think of another way of saying **hold on**.
Now turn to page 91 to check your answer.

Unit 3

get through (1)

What is the man doing?
Why?
Is the other number engaged?

Is the other man at home?
Is he answering the phone?
Make a sentence describing what happens when you phone someone and they are at home and the line isn't engaged.
Think of another way of saying **get through**.
Now turn to page 90 to check your answer.

stand for

What are the letters on the door?
What are the words the woman is thinking?
Make a sentence describing the relationship between the letters and the words.
Think of another way of saying **stand for**.
Now turn to page 95 to check your answer.

Complete these sentences using the six verbs from this unit. Use each verb only once.

1 The Gas Board have _____ our gas supply because we haven't paid our bill.
2 The telephone operator asked me to _____ while she dialled the number for me.
3 The letters U.S.A. _____ the United States of America.
4 Robert waited while the telephone operator _____ the call he was waiting for.
5 Joan couldn't _____ to her parents because the line was engaged.
6 The examiner asked Colin to _____ because he couldn't hear him.

Replace the words in italics by the words in brackets. Change the word order if necessary.

EXAMPLE   I'll put *her* through now. (Mrs Clarke)
       I'll put Mrs Clarke through now.

1 The Water Board cut off *our water supply*. (it)
2 Please put through *Mr Dodd's call*. (it)
3 The chairman cut *him* off in the middle of his speech. (John)

Fill the space with a preposition where necessary.

1 I was put through _____ central office.
2 Mr Gunn's secretary put through _____ his call to America.
3 I can't get through _____ London.

Complete the passage using **cut off/stand for/get through**.

The Electricity Board sent me a card with a red cross on it. I didn't know what the red cross _____ so I decided to phone the Electricity Board and ask them. When I _____ I was told the red cross meant that I would be _____ if I didn't pay my bill immediately.

Complete the passage using **speak up/put through/hold on**.

Ask Mr Ford to _____ and _____ him _____ when I finish the call on the other line. Mr Ford's a bit deaf so you'll have to _____ when you tell him.

Use the verbs in brackets to reply to the following.
· EXAMPLE He's got a very soft voice. (speak up)
POSSIBLE REPLY He'll have to **speak up** when he makes his speech.

1 Look at this symbol. (stand for)
2 Have you got your ticket? (hold on)
3 I turned on the tap but there was no water. (cut off)
4 I'd like extension 20, please. (put through)
5 Why didn't you phone me last night? (get through)
6 What did she say? (speak up)

Unit 4

break down (1)

What is happening?
Does the man look happy?
Is the car going well?

Does the man look happy now?
Is the car going well?
Make a sentence describing what has happened to the car.
Think of another way of saying **break down**.
Now turn to page 86 to check your answer.

break up (1)

Where do you think they are?
What is happening?
Do they look happy?

Do they look happy now?
Why do you think the man is carrying suitcases?
Make a sentence describing what has happened to their marriage.
Think of another way of saying **break up**.
Now turn to page 87 to check your answer.

break off

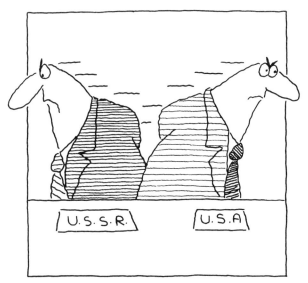

Where do the men come from?
Where do you think they are?
What are they doing?
Why do you think they are having talks?

What are they doing?
Do you think they are going to continue their talks?
Make a sentence describing what has happened to the talks.
Think of another way of saying **break off**.
Now turn to page 86 to check your answer.

make up (1)

What are they doing?
Do you think they are happy?

Are they still quarrelling?
Make a sentence describing what they are doing.
Think of another way of saying **make up**.
Now turn to page 93 to check your answer.

Unit 4

make up for

Where is the woman in picture one?
What is she doing?
Who do you think she is waiting for?
What time is it?
Is she still waiting in picture two?
How do you think she feels?
What time is it?
Who do you think she is with in picture three?
What is he giving her?
Make a sentence describing why he is giving her the bunch of flowers.
Think of another way of saying **make up for**.
Now turn to page 93 to check your answer.

fall out

What are the men doing?
Do you think they are enjoying themselves?

What is happening?
Do you think they are still enjoying themselves?
Make a sentence describing what they have done?
Think of another way of saying **fall out**.
Now turn to page 89 to check your answer.

Complete these sentences using the six verbs from this unit. Use each verb only once.

1 Julia decided that she was too young to get married so she _____ her engagement to Ian.
2 Our family _____ after our parents were divorced.
3 Why don't you two stop fighting and _____!
4 Jim apologized to his boss for being late and promised to _____ it by working an extra hour.
5 That new washing machine was a waste of money! It's always _____.
6 Paul and his sister were always _____ when they were young.

Fill the space with a preposition where necessary.

1 Jill made up _____ her boyfriend.
2 Jill made up _____ wasting time.
3 George and Sam fell out _____ money.

Replace the words in italics by the words in brackets. Change the word order if necessary.
EXAMPLE Ron fell out with *her*. (Sue)
            Ron fell out with Sue.

1 They made *it* up. (their quarrel)
2 They broke off *peace talks*. (them)
3 Alf fell out with *his brother*. (him)
4 My mother-in-law broke up *my marriage*. (it)
5 I'll make up for *my mistake*. (it)

Complete the passage using **make up/make up for/break off**.

Nina was very upset with Neil when he forgot her birthday. She told him that she wanted to _____ their engagement. Neil apologized and told her he would _____ forgetting her birthday by buying her a special gift. Nina accepted his apology and they kissed and _____.

Complete the passage using **break down/fall out/break up**.

Everything went wrong for Steve last month. His marriage _____, his car _____ and he _____ with his boss.

Use the verbs in brackets to reply to the following.
EXAMPLE I'm sorry I shouted at you. (make up)
POSSIBLE REPLY Why don't we **make up** and forget it.

1 This book is mine not yours! (fall out)
2 Howard and Jane are always quarrelling. (break up)
3 Do you want me to go away? (make up)
4 I put twenty pence in the coffee machine but I didn't get any coffee. (break down)
5 I'm sorry I forgot your birthday. (make up for)
6 Do you still want to marry me? (break off)

Unit 5

drop in

What is the woman doing?

What is she doing now?
What is her friend doing?
Do you think her friend is
expecting her?

Is her friend pleased to see her?
What do you think is going to
happen next?
Look at picture one and make a
sentence describing what the
woman decided to do.
Think of another way of saying
drop in.
Now turn to page 89 to check your
answer.

run into

What are they doing?
What do you think is going to happen next?

Do you think they know each other?
Do you think they expected to see each other?
Make a sentence describing what has just
happened to them.
Think of another way of saying **run into**.
Now turn to page 94 to check your answer.

come into

What is happening in picture one? Does the man in bed look well?
Why do you think the man with him looks so sad?
What has the old man got next to his bed?
What has happened to the old man in picture two?
Where do you think the old man is in picture three?
Why do you think both men look happy?
What did the old man do for the young man?
Make a sentence describing what happened to the young man when the old man died.
Think of another way of saying **come into**.

Now turn to page 88 to check your answer.

run in

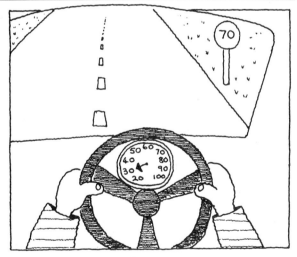

What is the man on the left doing?
Where is he?

What is he doing now?
What is the speed limit?
How fast is he driving?
Is his car new?
Make a sentence describing why he is driving his new car so slowly?
Think of another way of saying **run in**.

Now turn to page 94 to check your answer.

Unit 5

come across

Describe the man.
What is happening?
What can he see?

What has he found?
Did he expect to find it?
Make a sentence describing how he found the wallet.
Think of another way of saying **come across**.
Now turn to page 88 to check your answer.

get round (1)

What are they trying to do?
Can they do it?

Can they move it now?
How?
Make a sentence describing what they did about their problem.
Think of another way of saying **get round**.
Now turn to page 90 to check your answer.

Complete these sentences using the six verbs from this unit. Use each verb only once.

1 You should drive slowly while you are _____ your new car.
2 Mike _____ an old photograph as he was tidying the drawer.
3 Sarah _____ a lot of money when her grandfather died.
4 I think I'll _____ to see Paul on my way home.
5 We could _____ the problem by borrowing some money.
6 I _____ an old friend at the cinema.

Complete this sentence with verbs from this unit. There is more than one possible answer. Give all possible answers.

Sam _____ Tom while shopping in London.

Fill the space with a suitable word.

1 Why don't we drop in _____ Jack.
2 Why don't we drop in _____ see him.

Replace the words in italics by the words in brackets. Change the word order if necessary.
EXAMPLE I came across *it*. (an old book)
        I came across an old book.

1 I came into *a million pounds*. (it)
2 Norman ran into *her*. (Carol)
3 He's running in *his car*. (it)
4 Let's drop in on *Alec*. (him)
5 How can we get round *it*? (the problem)
6 Where did you come across *the vase*? (it)

Complete the passage using **run into/get round/run in**.

Don was invited to his friend's wedding, but he didn't have a suit. He _____ the problem by borrowing a suit from his brother. On the day of the wedding he couldn't take his car because he was still _____ it _____, so he decided to go by train. On his way to the station he _____ the bride's parents.

Complete the passage using **come into/drop in/come across**.

I was looking at an old address book when I _____ the address of a relative I hadn't seen for many years. I decided to _____ on him and see how he was. When I arrived at his house I was told that he had died and I had _____ all his possessions.

Use the verbs in brackets to reply to the following.
EXAMPLE Why are you driving so slowly? (run in)
POSSIBLE REPLY Because I'm **running in** my new car.

1 We'd love to see you. (drop in)
2 Where did you find that ring? (come across)
3 Where did you see Ron? (run into)
4 What's wrong with the car? (run in)
5 The main road is blocked! (get round)
6 Where did you get all this money? (come into)

Unit 6

break out in

Describe this man.
Do you think he looks well?

Do you think he looks well now?
Why not?
Make a sentence describing what has happened to
the man.
Think of another way of saying **break out in**.
Now turn to page 87 to check your answer.

break down (2)

Does this man look happy?

Does he look happy now?
What is he doing?
Do you think he is in control of his emotions?
Make a sentence describing what has happened to
him.
Think of another way of saying **break down**.
Now turn to page 86 to check your answer.

go down

Do you think this man is happy?
Why not?
Why do you think his cheek is swollen?

Is his cheek still swollen?
Make a sentence describing what has happened to his swollen cheek.
Think of another way of saying **go down**.
Now turn to page 90 to check your answer.

pass out

Does this man look well?
What do you think is wrong with him?

Is he still standing?
Is he still conscious?
Make a sentence describing what has happened to the man.
Think of another way of saying **pass out**.
Now turn to page 93 to check your answer.

Unit 6

come round/come to

What do you think has happened to the man lying on the ground?
Is he conscious?

Is he still unconscious?
Make a sentence describing what has happened to the man lying on the ground.
Think of another way of saying **come round/come to**.
Now turn to page 88 to check your answer.

get over

Where do you think they are? Why?
Why do you think the man is in bed?
Does he look well?

Is he still in bed?
Does he look better?
Where do you think he is going?
Make a sentence describing what has happened to the man.
Think of another way of saying **get over**.
Now turn to page 89 to check your answer.

Complete these sentences using the six verbs from this unit. Use each verb only once.

1 Alma took many years to _____ the death of her husband.
2 Peter _____ when he heard that he had won a million pounds.
3 Joan _____ a pink rash all over her body after eating rhubarb pie.
4 The unconscious woman _____ when we sprinkled some water on her face.
5 My swollen ankle _____ after I put some ice on it.
6 Nick _____ because he couldn't cope with the pressure of his job.

Replace the words in italics in the following passage with suitable verbs from this unit.

It is amazing how quickly people can *recover from* difficult periods in their lives. Last year my friend, Jack, started having problems with his job. Eventually the pressure became too much for him and he *became mentally ill* and had to go into a psychiatric hospital. When his mother heard what had happened to him she *lost control of her emotions* and wept. His father was very worried and *became covered by* a nervous rash. Fortunately Jack *overcame* his illness and was able to leave the hospital after a few weeks and return to his family.

Complete the passage using **come round** or **come to/break out in/break down**.

Last week I was attacked by two men. I _____ a cold sweat when one of them threatened me with a knife. When the other one punched me I _____ and cried. Finally one of them hit me on the head and knocked me unconscious. I didn't _____ for at least five minutes.

Complete the passage using **get over/pass out/go down**.

The front tyre of my bicycle kept _____ so I decided to _____ the problem by buying a new one. When I went to the shop to buy one I nearly _____ when I discovered how expensive they were.

Use the verbs in brackets to reply to the following.
EXAMPLE What happens when you get measles? (break out in)
POSSIBLE REPLY You **break out in** spots.

1 What happened when you hit your head on the wall? (pass out)
2 How long were you away from work after your heart attack? (get over)
3 How long were you unconscious? (come round/come to)
4 What did she do when she heard the terrible news? (break down)
5 How did you know he was frightened? (break out in)
6 The bruise on your head looks painful. (go down)

Unit 7

work out

What subject do you think this boy is studying?
Has he found the answer to his sum yet?
Make a sentence describing what he is doing in order to find the answer.
Think of another way of saying **work out**.
Now turn to page 96 to check your answer.

point out

What are they looking at?
Do you think the man is trying to show the woman something?
What do you think he is showing her?
Make a sentence describing what the man is doing with his right hand.
Think of another way of saying **point out**.
Now turn to page 93 to check your answer.

make out (1)

What is the man holding? Why?
Do you think he is looking at the thing on the horizon?
Do you think he can see what it is?

Do you think he can see what the thing is now?
What is it?
Can he see it clearly?
Make a sentence describing what the man is trying to do with his binoculars in the two pictures.
Think of another way of saying **make out**.
Now turn to page 92 to check your answer.

think over

What is the time?
What game is the man playing?
Do you think he is going to make a move?

What is the time now?
How long has the man been considering his next move?
Make a sentence describing what the man has been doing for the last five hours.
Think of another way of saying **think over**.
Now turn to page 96 to check your answer.

Unit 7

come up with

Can the man and woman be together?
What's the problem?
Does the man know how to solve the problem?

What is his idea?
Make a sentence describing how the man found a solution to the problem.
Think of another way of saying **come up with**.
Now turn to page 88 to check your answer.

make up (2)

Is the alarm clock ringing?
Is the man sleeping?

Is the man still sleeping?
Why do you think he looks so worried?

Do you think he is late for work?
Is he telling his boss that he overslept?
What is he telling her?
Is it true?
Make a sentence describing how the man got his excuse.
Think of another way of saying **make up**.
Now turn to page 93 to check your answer.

Complete these sentences using the six verbs from this unit. Use each verb only once.

1 I find it difficult to _____ original ideas.
2 Jane used an electronic calculator to _____ the maths problem.
3 You can't believe a word he says, he's always _____ stories!
4 Why don't you _____ my suggestion before you make a decision.
5 Our guide _____ the Houses of Parliament on our trip down the Thames.
6 Jeff couldn't _____ the address because it was so badly written.

Complete these sentences with verbs from this unit. Each sentence has more than one possible answer. Give all possible answers.

1 I'm going to _____ the problem.
2 I can't _____ where he is.

Replace the words in italics by the words in brackets. Change the word order if necessary.
EXAMPLE John worked out *a plan*. (it)
          John worked it out.

1 Think *it* over. (the proposal)
2 She came up with *a suggestion*. (it)
3 He worked out *the details*. (them)
4 She made *it* up. (the story about the man in the red coat)
5 She pointed out *the man*. (him)
6 I can't make out *the number*. (it)

Complete the passage using **think over/make out/make up**.

Ben's a very strange man; I can't _____ him _____ at all. He _____ silly poems and if you ask him what they mean he locks himself in his room to _____ his reply.

Complete the passage using **work out/come up with/point out**.

My solicitor has _____ some difficulties in your proposal, so we'll need some time to _____ them _____ However, I'm sure we'll be able to _____ an acceptable compromise.

Use the verbs in brackets to reply to the following.
EXAMPLE Where did you find that poem? (make up)
POSSIBLE REPLY I didn't find it, I **made** it **up**.

1 The basic plan is good, but what about the details? (work out)
2 What did he just say? (make out)
3 Did you see Buckingham Palace? (point out)
4 Who made the suggestion? (come up with)
5 I don't know whether to accept the offer. (think over)
6 Is your explanation true? (make up)

Unit 8

hold up (1)

Is the traffic moving?
Why not?
Make a sentence describing what the accident is doing to the movement of traffic.
Think of another way of saying **hold up**.
Now turn to page 91 to check your answer.

see off

Where are they?
Why do you think they are there?

Where is the boy now?
What is he doing?
Make a sentence describing what his father is doing.
Think of another way of saying **see off**.
Now turn to page 94 to check your answer.

drop off (1)

Do you think the car is moving?
What is the man doing?

Is the car still moving?
Are they still in the car?
Make a sentence describing what the driver is doing for his passenger.
Think of another way of saying **drop off**.
Now turn to page 89 to check your answer.

take off (1)

Is the aeroplane moving?
Is it on the ground?

Is the aeroplane still on the ground?
Is the journey beginning or ending?
Make a sentence describing what the aeroplane is doing.
Think of another way of saying **take off**.
Now turn to page 95 to check your answer.

Unit 8

pick up

What is the man by the roadside doing?
Do you think the car is going to stop for him?

Has the car stopped?
Is the man going to get in?
Make a sentence describing what the driver is doing for the hitchhiker.
Think of another way of saying **pick up**.
Now turn to page 93 to check your answer.

set off

Why do you think the young man has a rucksack on his back?
Do you think his journey is beginning or ending?
Do you think his parents are going with him?
Make a sentence describing what the young man is doing.
Think of another way of saying **set off**.
Now turn to page 95 to check your answer.

Complete these sentences using the six verbs from this unit. Use each verb only once.

1 When my brother flew to France we drove him to the airport to _____ him _____.
2 We watched the expedition as it _____ on its trip to China.
3 The aeroplane _____ and disappeared behind the clouds.
4 My father _____ me _____ outside the station and drove me home.
5 I'll _____ you _____ at the station and you can catch the London train.
6 I'm sorry I'm late. I was _____ in a traffic jam.

Change these sentences into the passive.
EXAMPLE The rescue boat picked up the shipwrecked sailors.
The shipwrecked sailors were picked up by the rescue boat.

1 Bad weather held up the start of the race.
2 My father dropped me off.

Replace the words in italics by the words in brackets. Change the word order if necessary.
EXAMPLE Jeff picked up *the hitchhiker*. (him)
Jeff picked him up.

1 We saw *him* off. (Steve)
2 Joe dropped *them* off. (his daughter and her friend)
3 The power failure held up *the train*. (it)
4 They picked *her* up. (Jane)

Complete the passage using **hold up/pick up/set off**.

I'll _____ you _____ at 7 a.m. tomorrow, and then we'll _____ on our trip together. Do all your packing tonight so that nothing _____ us _____ in the morning.

Complete the passage using **see off/take off/drop off**.

If you _____ me _____ at the airport on your way to work, I'll be able to _____ them _____. Their plane doesn't _____ until lunchtime.

Fill the space with a preposition where necessary.

1 We set off _____ our journey.
2 We set off _____ dawn.
3 We set off _____ an hour ago.
4 We set off _____ Italy.

Use the verbs in brackets to reply to the following.
EXAMPLE What time are you leaving? (set off)
POSSIBLE REPLY I'm going to **set off** at five.

1 Why are you going to the airport? (see off)
2 What's that in the distance?(take off)
3 When did Jim go to work? (set off)
4 Why are you late? (hold up)
5 How are you getting home? (pick up)
6 Where do you want me to take you? (drop off)

Unit 9

call off

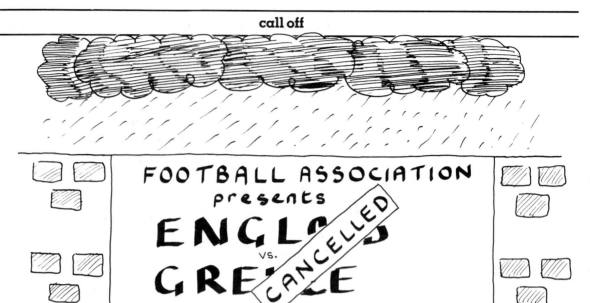

What is the poster advertising?
Which teams are playing?
What's the weather like?
Make a sentence describing what the Football Association did to the match because of the bad weather.
Think of another way of saying **call off**.
Now turn to page 87 to check your answer.

put off (1)

Where is the man?
What can you see by the sink?
Why do you think the man looks so unhappy?

Does he still look unhappy?
Do you think he is going to wash the dishes now?
Do you think he'll wash the dishes tomorrow?
Make a sentence describing what he is doing about the washing-up today.
Think of another way of saying **put off**.
Now turn to page 94 to check your answer.

be taken aback

What is he going to do?

What is behind the door?
Make a sentence describing the man's reaction to what he has found behind the door.
Think of another way of saying **be taken aback**.
Now turn to page 86 to check your answer.

be over

Describe the weather.

Is it still raining?
Is it still windy?
Make a sentence describing what has happened to the storm.
Think of another way of saying **be over**.
Now turn to page 86 to check your answer.

Unit 9

be off (1)

What is the poster advertising?
Make a sentence describing what has happened to the concert.
Think of another way of saying **be off**.
Now turn to page 86 to check your answer.

give out

Where are they?
What is the teacher holding?
Make a sentence describing what the teacher is doing with the books.
Think of another way of saying **give out**.
Now turn to page 90 to check your answer.

Complete these sentences using the six verbs from this unit. Use each verb only once.

1 The audience is leaving the theatre because the play _____.
2 My parents _____ by my unexpectedly bad examination result.
3 Dave and Sally had a terrible argument and decided to _____ their wedding.
4 Julia and Fred are very young, so they have decided to _____ their wedding for a few years.
5 The nurse _____ the tablets to the patients.
6 The wedding _____ because Deborah has decided not to marry Bill.

Change these sentences into the passive. Do not include the agent in your answer.
EXAMPLE They called the match off.
          The match was called off.

1 The man gave out the pamphlets.
2 The chairperson put off the next meeting until after Christmas.
3 The police called off the search.

Replace the words in italics by the words in brackets. Change the word order if necessary.
EXAMPLE They called off *the concert*. (it)
          They called it off.

1 Mother gave *them* out. (the sweets)
2 Jack put off *the cleaning*. (it)
3 Mr Smith called *it* off. (the meeting of the students' club)

Complete the passage using **give out/be over/be taken aback**.

I _____ when I saw a man _____ money in the street to passersby. By the time I reached him, his act of generosity _____ because he didn't have any money left!

Complete the passage using **call off/put off/be off**.

"_____ the lecture _____?"
"No, it hasn't been _____. They've just _____ it _____ until next week."

Use the verbs in brackets to reply to the following.
EXAMPLE What shall I do with these examination papers? (give out)
POSSIBLE REPLY **Give** them **out** to the students.

1 How did you feel when they told you the news? (be taken aback)
2 Has the meeting been cancelled? (put off)
3 The students have used all their paper. (give out)
4 People are leaving the cinema. (be over)
5 Why can't we go to the meeting tonight? (be off)
6 What do you think we should do about the business deal? (call off)

Unit 10

---

try on

Where do you think this man is?
What does he want to buy?
Does the hat in picture one fit him?
Does the hat in picture two fit him?
Do you think he'll buy the hat in picture three? Why?
Make a sentence describing what the man did in the three pictures to find a hat that fitted him.
Think of another way of saying **try on**.
Now turn to page 96 to check your answer.

---

wear out (1)

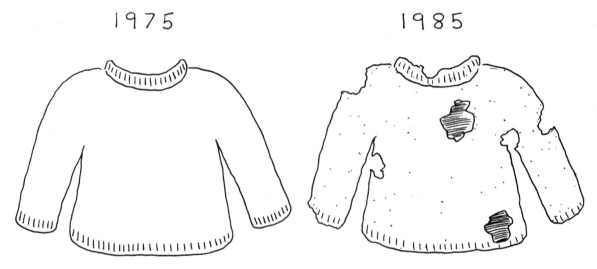

When did Paul buy this jumper?
Was it in good condition then?

How long has he had the jumper now?
Is it still in good condition?
Make a sentence describing what has happened to the jumper after ten years of use.
Think of another way of saying **wear out**.
Now turn to page 96 to check your answer.

---

do up (2)

What is he wearing?
Are there many buttons on it?

Make a sentence describing what the man is doing
to the buttons on his coat in the two pictures.
Think of another way of saying **do up**.
Now turn to page 88 to check your answer.

---

take off (2)

Make a sentence describing what the man is doing with his jacket in these
two pictures.
Think of another way of saying **take off**.
Now turn to page 95 to check your answer.

Unit 10

---
go with

Describe the man's jacket.
Describe his trousers.
Why do you think the man looks unhappy with them?

Describe the trousers the man is wearing now.
Does the man look happy?
Make a sentence describing the relationship between the jacket and trousers in this picture.
Think of another way of saying **go with**.
Now turn to page 91 to check your answer.

---
put on

Make a sentence describing what the boy is doing with the sweater in these two pictures.
Think of another way of saying **put on**.
Now turn to page 94 to check your answer.

Unit 10

Complete these sentences using the six verbs from this unit. Use each verb only once.

1 The zip on my new jacket doesn't _____ properly.
2 Every morning I get up and _____ my clothes.
3 Every night I _____ my clothes before I go to bed.
4 You should always _____ a new pair of shoes before you buy them.
5 Do you think this dress _____ the colour of my eyes?
6 Your shoes will _____ quickly if you play football in them!

Complete the sentences using the verbs in brackets.

1 (put on) My hands are cold, so _____
2 (take off) Before the doctor examined me, he _____
3 (go with) This wallpaper _____
4 (wear out) Cheap clothes _____
5 (try on) Before I buy it, I'd _____
6 (do up) I always have to help my little son to _____

Replace the words in italics by the words in brackets. Change the word order if necessary.
EXAMPLE Fred did up *the zip*. (it)
         Fred did it up.

1 I've worn *them* out. (my boots)
2 Joan took off *her cardigan*. (it)
3 This hat goes with *the dress*. (it)
4 Chris put *them* on. (his trousers)
5 Do *your shoelace* up. (it)
6 Can I try *it* on? (your new watch)

Complete the passage using **try on/put on/go with**.

I'll have to _____ my glasses _____ before I _____ the new suit or I won't be able to see if it _____ the colour of my hair.

Complete the passage using **do up/take off/wear out**.

Don't wear your new shoes all the time! _____ them _____ occasionally or you'll _____ them _____; and when you put them on, _____ them _____ properly.

Use the verbs in brackets to reply to the following.
EXAMPLE It's very cold tonight. (do up)
POSSIBLE REPLY You'll be warmer if you **do up** your jacket.

1 My jacket's full of holes. (wear out)
2 I really like your new skirt! (try on)
3 Why are you wearing my new trousers! (take off)
4 I can't reach the zip on the back of my dress. (do up)
5 I've bought you a new pair of earrings. (put on)
6 What shall I wear with my pink hat? (go with)

Unit 11

give (oneself) up (1)

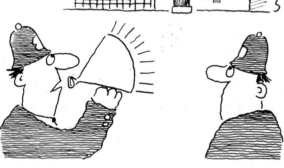

Why do you think the police have surrounded this house?
What kind of person do you think they are looking for?

Is the person they want still inside the house?
Do you think he is a policeman?
Why do you think he has his hands in the air?
Make a sentence describing what the man is doing.
Think of another way of saying **give (oneself) up**.
Now turn to page 90 to check your answer.

try out

What is the woman doing?
What is on the television?

Where is the woman now?
What is she buying?
Make a sentence describing what the woman decided to do after she saw the advertisement for 'Zap'.
Think of another way of saying **try out**.
Now turn to page 96 to check your answer.

give up (2)

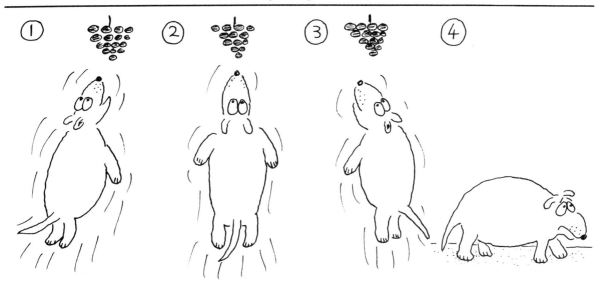

What do you think the dog is trying to do in the first three pictures?
Is it successful?
How do you think the dog feels in picture four?
Look at picture four and make a sentence describing what the dog has decided to do about trying to get the grapes.
Think of another way of saying **give up**.
Now turn to page 90 to check your answer.

catch on

Look at the boy on the left and describe his hairstyle.
What do you think the other boys think of his hairstyle?

What have the other boys done now?
Do they look pleased about it?
Do you think more boys will copy the hairstyle?
Look at both pictures again and make a sentence describing what is happening to the new hairstyle.
Think of another way of saying **catch on**.
Now turn to page 87 to check your answer.

Unit 11

What has the man got in his mouth?
What is he looking at?
Why do you think he looks so unhappy?

What is he doing with his cigarette now?
Does he still look unhappy?
Make a sentence describing what the man decided to do after he saw the poster.
Think of another way of saying **give up**.
Now turn to page 90 to check your answer.

drop off (2)

What is the man doing? Why?

What is he doing now?
Make a sentence describing what has happened to the man.
Think of another way of saying **drop off**.
Now turn to page 89 to check your answer.

Complete these sentences using the six verbs from this unit. Use each verb only once. If the answer is **give up** say if it is (1), (2) or (3).

1 The escaped convict _____ himself _____ to the police.
2 I _____; this maths problem is too difficult for me.
3 Peter _____ eating sweets because the dentist told him they were bad for his teeth.
4 Ben asked the salesman if he could _____ the car before deciding whether to buy it.
5 It's a great new product and the sale's figures show that it's _____ very quickly.
6 Harry _____ on the train and missed his station.

Choose words from the box to fill the gaps. Use each word only once.

themselves	playing
the	to
trying	drinking

1 Don't give up, keep _____.
2 Rachel gave up playing _____ piano because she couldn't afford the lessons.
3 The Todd brothers gave _____ up _____ the authorities.
4 Colin wants to give up _____ alcohol because it's bad for his health.
5 Sam gave up _____ the guitar when he broke his arm.

Complete the passage using **give up (3)/catch on/try out**.

Jogging is beginning to _____ in a big way, so I've decided to _____ it _____ and _____ tennis.

Complete the passage using **drop off/give up (1)/give up (2)**.

The escaped prisoner was surrounded by the police, but he still refused to _____ himself _____. After twenty hours, however, he had to _____ his struggle because he kept _____.

Use the verbs in brackets to reply to the following.
EXAMPLE I can't swim any further. (give up (2))
POSSIBLE REPLY Don't **give up** yet, we're almost there.

1 What do you think of my idea? (catch on)
2 What did the murderer do? (give oneself up (1))
3 What happens when grandfather sits in front of the television? (drop off)
4 Did your expedition get to the top of the mountain? (give up (2))
5 Would you like a whisky? (give up (3))
6 Can I have the job? (try out)

Unit 12

get round (2)

What do you think the boy wants?
Do you think his father wants him
to have them?

What is happening now?

Where are they going?
Do you think the boy is going to
get what he wants?
Make a sentence describing what
the boy did to his father in picture
two.
Think of another way of saying **get
round**.

Now turn to page 90 to check your
answer.

go through

Where are they?
What is happening? Why?

What is happening now?
Why do you think the man on the right looks so
unhappy?
Make a sentence describing what the customs
officer is doing to the suitcase and its contents.
Think of another way of saying **go through**.

Now turn to page 91 to check your answer.

mistake for

What time of the day do you think it is?
What is the man holding?
Is it switched on?
What does he think he can see?
Does he look happy?

Is the torch switched on now?
Can he see a snake or a piece of rope?
Does he look frightened?
Look at picture one and make a sentence describing how the man confused the piece of rope and the snake.
Think of another way of saying **mistake for**.
Now turn to page 93 to check your answer.

be off (2)

What is the man holding?
What do you think he is going to do with it?

What has he just done?
Make a sentence describing the condition of the egg.
Think of another way of saying **be off**.
Now turn to page 86 to check your answer.

Unit 12

---

take in

What can you see in the picture?
Are all the animals sheep?
Do the sheep look frightened?
Do you think they should be frightened? Why?
Make a sentence describing what the wolf has done to the sheep with his disguise.
Think of another way of saying **take in**.

Now turn to page 95 to check your answer.

---

give in

What are they doing?

Are they still fighting?
Do you think they both wanted to stop fighting?
Make a sentence describing why the fight stopped.
Think of another way of saying **give in**.

Now turn to page 90 to check your answer.

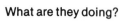

Complete these sentences using the six verbs from this unit. Use each verb only once.

1 Howard doesn't want to drive us to the station, but I know I can _____ him.
2 I _____ her _____ her sister because they're so much alike.
3 This meat smells awful; I think it _____.
4 I'd like you to _____ these accounts and see if you can find any mistakes.
5 Harry was _____ by the salesman's lies.
6 The industrial dispute lasted for many months because neither side would

_____.

Complete the sentences using the verbs in brackets.

1 (give in) Keep fighting, _____
2 (take in) Terry's promises _____
3 (get round) Stop trying to persuade me _____
4 (be off) This chicken smells bad, _____
5 (go through) Your homework is full of mistakes, _____
6 (mistake for) Colin was very drunk and he_____

Replace the words in italics by the words in brackets. Change the word order if necessary.
EXAMPLE The salesman took *Fred* in with his lies. (him)
        The salesman took him in with his lies.

1 Jake got round *his wife*. (her)
2 The trick took *them* in. (the tourists)
3 The police went through *their records*. (them)
4 I mistook *that man* for my father. (him)

Complete the passage using **go through/be off/take in**.

The fish I had in that restaurant _____. I was _____ by the notice on the door which read, 'Fresh fish daily'. Before I go out to eat again, I shall _____ my restaurant guide book very carefully first!

Complete the passage using **give in/get round/mistake for**.

Steve _____ Alma's kindness _____ love; he kept asking her to be his wife, but she refused to _____ and marry him. However hard he tried he couldn't _____ her.

Use the verbs in brackets to reply to the following.
EXAMPLE Why are you throwing that pie away? (be off)
POSSIBLE REPLY Because it**'s off**.

1 Why did you give him all your money? (take in)
2 Why did you say hello to that stranger? (mistake for)
3 Roy refuses to lend us the money. (get round)
4 Do you think we should continue our struggle? (give in)
5 Why don't you buy meat from that butcher? (be off)
6 What are you going to do with those files? (go through)

Unit 13

look up to

What is the man's job?
Does the boy look happy to see the man?
Do you think the boy would like to be a professional footballer?
Make a sentence describing how you think the boy feels about the man.
Think of another way of saying **look up to**.
Now turn to page 92 to check your answer.

cheer up

Does he look happy?

Does he look happy now?
Look at the two pictures and make a sentence
describing the change in how the man is feeling.
Think of another way of saying **cheer up**.
Now turn to page 88 to check your answer.

put (someone) off (2)

What is the man on the right trying to do?

Why is he having problems?

Make a sentence describing how the noise from the television is affecting him.

Think of another way of saying **put (someone) off**.

Now turn to page 94 to check your answer.

look down on

Do you think the man on the left is rich?

Why not?

What about the other man?

Do you think that the man on the right thinks he is better than the man on the left?

Make a sentence describing what you think the man on the right thinks of the other man.

Think of another way of saying **look down on**.

Now turn to page 92 to check your answer.

Unit 13

look forward to

Where is he?
What is he thinking about?
Is the thought making him happy?
Make a sentence describing how the man is feeling about leaving prison.
Think of another way of saying **look forward to**.
Now turn to page 92 to check your answer.

put up with

What are the children doing?
Do you think they are behaving well?
Would you like to be the man? Why not?
What would you do if you were the man?
Make a sentence describing how the man is reacting to the children.
Think of another way of saying **put up with**.
Now turn to page 94 to check your answer.

Complete these sentences using the six verbs from this unit. Use each verb only once.

1 The bad newspaper reviews _____ me _____ going to see the new film.
2 Last winter we had to _____ a lot of discomfort when our central heating system stopped working.
3 My parents _____ my boyfriend because he hasn't got a good job.
4 Children should _____ their parents.
5 Every year I _____ my summer holiday.
6 I expect this present will _____ her _____

Complete these sentences using the 'ing' form of the verb in brackets.
EXAMPLE The noise put Ron off _____ (read his book)
        The noise put Ron off reading his book.

1 I'm looking forward to _____ (meet him)
2 The bad weather put me off _____ (go for a walk)
3 We are looking forward to _____ (see him again)

Replace the words in italics by the words in brackets. Change the word order if necessary.
EXAMPLE Tom cheered *his sister* up. (her)
        Tom cheered her up.

1 My father is looking forward to *his retirement*. (it)
2 He put me off *the idea*. (it)
3 The invitation cheered *him* up. (Terry)
4 I don't know how you put up with *all your troubles*. (them)
5 They look down on *Peter*. (him)
6 We look up to *her*. (Sally)

Complete the passage using **put (someone) off/look up to/look down on**.

People _____ Mr Price because he is a dustman and they _____ Mr Brown because he is a bank manager. All this has _____ me _____ the idea of becoming a dustman.

Complete the passage using **cheer up/put up with/look forward to**.

Your brother is always complaining, I don't know how you _____ him. I'm really _____ the day when he _____ a bit.

Use the verbs in brackets to reply to the following.
EXAMPLE How do you feel about the party?
POSSIBLE REPLY I'm really **looking forward to** it.

1 Jeff looks very sad. (cheer up)
2 Why do you think Brian is a snob? (look down on)
3 My father-in-law is very rude. (put up with)
4 It should be a very exciting football match. (look forward to)
5 Why do you want me to stop talking? (put off)
6 What do you think of your father? (look up to)

Unit 14

soak up

Is there a mess?
Why do you think the man is holding a sponge?

Is there still a mess?
Make a sentence describing what the sponge did to the spilt milk.
Think of another way of saying **soak up**.
Now turn to page 95 to check your answer.

break up (2)

What are the boys doing?
Does their headmaster look pleased with them?

Are they still fighting? Why not?
Make a sentence describing what the headmaster did to their fight.
Think of another way of saying **break up**.
Now turn to page 87 to check your answer.

tell off

Do you think the boy broke the window?
How do you think he broke it?
Does he look happy about it?

Does the boy's father look pleased with him?
Make a sentence describing what the man is doing to his son.
Think of another way of saying **tell off**.
Now turn to page 96 to check your answer.

beat up

Do you think the bearded man is hurt?
Make a sentence describing what the other men are doing to the bearded man.
Think of another way of saying **beat up**.
Now turn to page 86 to check your answer.

Unit 14

go for

Does the dog look friendly?

Make a sentence describing what the dog is doing to the man.
Think of another way of saying **go for**.
Now turn to page 90 to check your answer.

calm down

How do you think this man feels?

Do you think he is still as angry as he was in picture one?

Is he angry now?
Make a sentence describing what happened to the angry man in picture two and picture three.
Think of another way of saying **calm down**.
Now turn to page 87 to check your answer.

Complete these sentences using the six verbs from this unit. Use each verb only once.

1 The meeting _____ at ten o'clock.
2 The boys _____ the old man and took his money.
3 My boss _____ me _____ for being late.
4 _____, there's nothing to worry about.
5 The carpet _____ the wine.
6 The madman _____ John with a knife.

Complete these sentences using the 'ing' form of the verb in brackets.
EXAMPLE I told him off for _____ (not do his homework)
           I told him off for not doing his homework.

1 The teacher told her off for _____ (be rude)
2 The teacher told him off for _____ (eat in class)
3 I was told off for _____ (not help my mother)

Replace the words in italics by the words in brackets. Change the word order if necessary.
EXAMPLE They beat up *my friend*. (him)
           They beat him up.

1 I told *her* off. (Janet)
2 Let's beat *him* up. (George)
3 The protesters broke up *the meeting*. (it)
4 The student soaked *it* up. (a lot of information)
5 The dog went for *the postman*. (him)
6 This glass of whisky will calm *him* down. (Phillip)

Complete the passage using **go for/break up/calm down**.

Last night's meeting _____ in disorder when a man from the audience _____ the chairman with a knife. It took us twenty minutes to _____ the man _____ and take his knife from him.

Complete the passage using **tell off/soak up/beat up**.

Last week Roy had a fight with three older boys. He _____ a lot of punishment as they _____ him _____ and he had to go to hospital. When his mother visited him she cried and _____ him _____ for fighting.

Use the verbs in brackets to reply to the following.
EXAMPLE Sue is very upset. (calm down)
POSSIBLE REPLY Don't worry, I'll **calm** her **down**.

1 Your son was very rude to his teacher. (tell off)
2 I'm really worried about my exam. (calm down)
3 What happened when the police arrived at the party? (break up)
4 How did Colin get that black eye? (beat up)
5 Why are you looking so frightened? (go for)
6 Why is this cloth damp? (soak up)

Unit 15

---

tear up

What is the man doing in picture one?
Does he look happy?
Make a sentence describing what he is doing to the letter in picture two and picture three.
Think of another way of saying **tear up**.
Now turn to page 96 to check your answer.

---

check in

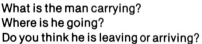

What is the man carrying?
Where is he going?
Do you think he is leaving or arriving?

What is he holding?
Make a sentence describing what the man is doing at the reception desk.
Think of another way of saying **check in**.
Now turn to page 88 to check your answer.

make out (2)

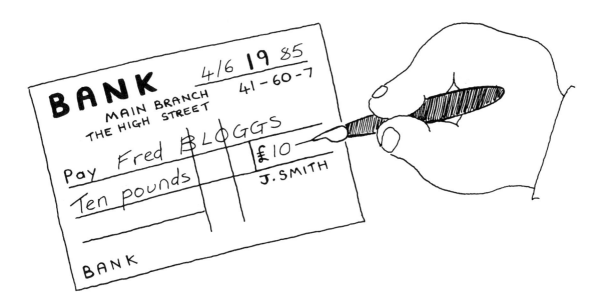

Who is holding the pen?
Make a sentence describing what John Smith is doing with the cheque.
Think of another way of saying **make out**.
Now turn to page 93 to check your answer.

take up

What is the man reading?
Where is the evening class?
Does he look interested in the evening class?

What is he holding?
Do you think he is going to go into the College?
Make a sentence describing what he is going to do inside the College.
Think of another way of saying **take up**.
Now turn to page 95 to check your answer.

Unit 15

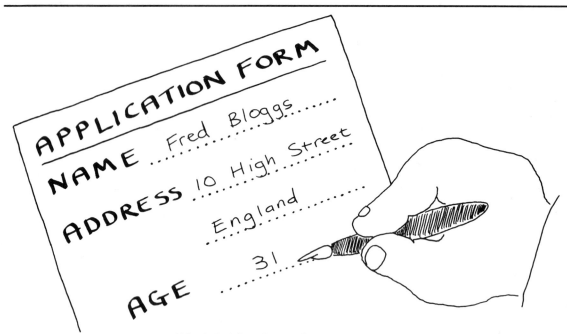

Who is holding the pen?
Make a sentence describing what Fred Bloggs is doing with the form.
Think of another way of saying **fill in**.
Now turn to page 89 to check your answer.

---

take down

What do you think has happened to the cars?
What do you think the man on the left is doing?
Make a sentence describing what the policeman is doing as the man is telling him about the accident.
Think of another way of saying **take down**.
Now turn to page 95 to check your answer.

Complete these sentences using the six verbs from this unit. Use each verb only once.

1 Please _____ the cheque to Bloggs Brothers Ltd.
2 The secretary _____ what her boss said in the meeting.
3 It's a good idea to _____ early so that you get a good seat on the plane.
4 My little son _____ my newspaper, so I had to buy another one.
5 I _____ the violin when I was seven years old.
6 You'll have to _____ this form before we give you the money.

Complete these sentences, using the 'ing' form where necessary.
EXAMPLE Jack took up _____ (French)
        Jack took up French.
EXAMPLE Jack took up _____ (fish)
        Jack took up fishing.

1 Mike took up _____ (box)
2 Sue took up _____ (knit)
3 Bill took up _____ (woodwork)
4 Sally took up _____ (tennis)

Replace the words in italics by the words in brackets. Change the word order if necessary.
EXAMPLE He tore up *the piece of paper*. (it)
        He tore it up.

1 He filled *it* in. (the questionnaire)
2 I made *it* out. (a cheque for forty pounds)
3 I took down *her telephone number*. (it)
4 My son took up *stamp-collecting*. (it)
5 She tore *it* up. (the letter from her boyfriend)

Complete the passage using **take down/make out/take up**.

I decided to _____ the piano when I saw an advertisement outside the local music college. I _____ details of the course in my diary and when I arrived home I _____ a cheque to cover the cost of tuition and sent it to the college.

Complete the passage using **tear up/fill in/check in**.

When I _____ at the Airline International desk they gave me a questionnaire and asked me to _____ it _____ after my flight. They told me that the information was used to improve their service. I thought it was a waste of time, so I _____ my questionnaire.

Use the verbs in brackets to reply to the following.
EXAMPLE I'm bored with playing tennis. (take up)
POSSIBLE REPLY Why don't you **take up** squash instead.

1 Why are you in such a hurry to get to the airport? (check in)
2 How much do you want? (make out)
3 What's happened to my magazine? (tear up)
4 I feel really unhealthy. (take up)
5 Why have you got that notebook? (take down)
6 How can I get that job? (fill in)

Unit 16

take over

①

②

③

What is the manager's name?
Is he old or young?
Is he talking to a young man?

Is Mr Jones still sitting behind his desk?
What is he doing?

Is Mr Jones still the manager?
Do you think he has retired?
Why?
Make a sentence describing what has happened to Mr Brown.
Think of another way of saying **take over**.
Now turn to page 95 to check your answer.

pass away/pass on/pass over

What can you see in this picture?
Make a sentence describing what happened to Fred Bloggs in 1985.
Think of another way of saying **pass away/pass on/pass over**.
Now turn to page 93 to check your answer.

turn into

What is the princess holding?
What is she doing to it?

Make a sentence describing what has happened to the frog.
Think of another way of saying **turn into**.
Now turn to page 96 to check your answer.

wear off

What is wrong with this man?
What is he drinking?

Is the pain in his foot as bad as it was in picture one?

Make a sentence describing what is happening to the pain in the three pictures.
Think of another way of saying **wear off**.
Now turn to page 96 to check your answer.

Unit 16

brush up

Where are they?
Where is the man on the right from?
Where is the man on the left from?
Do you think the man on the left knows any French?
Where do you think he learnt French?

Do you think the Englishman's French is good?
Do you think he can understand what the Frenchman is saying to him?
Do you think his visit to the business conference is a success?

Make a sentence describing what the Englishman is doing now.
Think of another way of saying **brush up**.
Now turn to page 87 to check your answer.

die out

What can you see in the picture?

Make a sentence describing what happened to the dinosaurs.
Think of another way of saying **die out**.
Now turn to page 88 to check your answer.

Complete these sentences using the six verbs from this unit. Use each verb only once.

1 I'm going to _____ my spare bedroom _____ a bathroom.
2 Paul wants to _____ his knowledge of modern history.
3 The government wants to _____ the country's computer industry.
4 The effects of the drug took some time to _____.
5 These rare animals will _____ if people don't stop hunting them.
6 I'm sorry to hear that your grandmother _____.

Complete the sentences using the verbs in brackets.

1 (brush up) I'm taking private lessons _____
2 (pass away/on/over) How many years is it since _____
3 (wear off) The smell of the paint _____
4 (turn into) The magician took my handkerchief and _____
5 (take over) I'm going on holiday for three weeks so I'd like you to _____
6 (die out) If people were allowed to shoot as many elephants as they wanted

_____

Complete the passage using **die out/wear off/brush up**.

Last week I decided to _____ my knowledge of natural history by going to the library and borrowing a few books on the subject. In one of the books I learned that many kinds of animals and birds are _____ because of the terrible things people do to them. The shock of this discovery took a long time to _____.

Complete the passage using **turn into/pass away** or **pass on** or **pass over/take over**.

Young Eric _____ when his poor father _____. His father's death has _____ him _____ a much stronger person.

Use the words in brackets to reply to the following.
EXAMPLE What have they done to the old cinema? (turn into)
POSSIBLE REPLY They've **turned** it **into** a supermarket.

1 Why do you look so sad? (pass away/pass on/pass over)
2 Why did you buy that book? (brush up)
3 Who is going to be chairman when Tim leaves? (take over)
4 What has happened to that ancient custom? (die out)
5 What are you going to do with your old garage? (turn into)
6 Are you still feeling uncomfortable? (wear off)

Unit 17

get away with

Why do you think he is wearing a mask.
What do you think he has just done?
What do you think is in his sack?

Where is he now?
Do you think he is enjoying the money he stole?
Do you think he is lucky? Why?
Has he been punished for his crime?
Make a sentence describing what happened to him after robbing the bank.
Think of another way of saying **get away with**.

Now turn to page 89 to check your answer.

let down

What time is it?
What is the man holding?
Who do you think he is waiting for?

What time is it now?
How long has he been waiting?
Has his girlfriend arrived yet?
Does he look pleased?
Make a sentence describing what the woman has done to the man.
Think of another way of saying **let down**.

Now turn to page 91 to check your answer.

get away

What are the guards doing?

What is the prisoner doing?

Make a sentence describing what the prisoner is doing now.
Think of another way of saying **get away**.
Now turn to page 89 to check your answer.

own up

Why is the teacher angry?
Do you think he drew the picture on the board?
Who do you think drew the picture?
Make a sentence describing what you think the boy with the raised arm is going to do.
Think of another way of saying **own up**.
Now turn to page 93 to check your answer.

Unit 17

let out

Make a sentence describing what the guard is doing for the prisoner.
Think of another way of saying **let out**.
Now turn to page 91 to check your answer.

let off

Where are they?
What does the man on the left do?
Why is the other man wearing handcuffs?
What do you think the criminal is talking about?

Is the judge sending him to prison?
Make a sentence describing what the judge is doing to him.
Think of another way of saying **let off**.
Now turn to page 91 to check your answer.

Complete these sentences using each verb from this unit only once.

1 The police chased the robber, but he _____.
2 Open the back door and _____ the cat _____.
3 The headmaster was going to punish the boy, but decided to _____ him _____ with a warning.
4 That student never does any homework, I don't know how he _____ it.
5 Phil _____ to the crime.
6 My friend _____ me _____ by not helping me when I needed him.

Replace the words in italics by the words in brackets. Change the word order if necessary.
EXAMPLE The police let *him* out. (Joe)
      The police let Joe out.

1 The boss let *Sue* off. (her)
2 I let *my friend* down. (him)
3 Who let *the cat* out? (it)
4 She got away with *the crime*. (it)

Complete these sentences, using the 'ing' form where necessary.
EXAMPLE Jack got away with _____ (the bank robbery)
      Jack got away with the bank robbery.
EXAMPLE Jack got away with _____ (rob the bank)
      Jack got away with robbing the bank.

1 Mother let me off _____ (wash the dishes)
2 Sally owned up to _____ (the lie)
3 Dan got away with _____ (tell a lie)

Complete the passage using **let out/get away/let off.**

On Friday afternoon my teacher _____ me _____ the last lesson so that I could go fishing. I was really excited and felt like a man who had just been _____ of prison. Unfortunately, my fishing trip wasn't very successful because all the fish I tried to catch managed to _____.

Complete the passage using **own up/get away with/let down.**

You shouldn't have forged your father's signature on that cheque, you'll never _____ it. Don't _____ your father _____, go to him now and _____.

Use the verbs in brackets to reply to the following.
EXAMPLE Are you going to punish me? (let off)
POSSIBLE REPLY No, I'm going to **let** you **off.**

1 Where is the thief? (get away)
2 Why are you looking so unhappy? (let down)
3 How do you know that Howard stole the money? (own up)
4 Did the judge send Sam to prison? (let off)
5 Did the boss know you lied about being late? (get away with)
6 How did the dog get into the garden? (let out)

Unit 18

turn down

Who is the man waiting to see?
Why?

Where is he now?
Who is he talking to?
Do you think he wants the job?

Does he look pleased with his interview?
Do you think he got the job?
Make a sentence describing what the manager did to him.
Think of another way of saying **turn down**.
Now turn to page 96 to check your answer.

drop out

What are they doing?
Is the man on the right enjoying himself? Why not?
Is he still in the race?
Make a sentence describing what the man on the right has just done.
Think of another way of saying **drop out**.
Now turn to page 89 to check your answer.

carry out

What orders is the sergeant giving the private?

Make a sentence describing what the private is doing about the orders.
Think of another way of saying **carry out**.
Now turn to page 87 to check your answer.

fall through

Where are they?
What kind of holiday is the man on the right booking?

What is happening?

Did he hurt himself when he fell down the steps of the travel agency?
What happened to him?
Make a sentence describing what happened to his plan to go on a skiing holiday.
Think of another way of saying **fall through**.
Now turn to page 89 to check your answer.

Unit 18

lay off

Why does the manager of Bloggs Ltd look so worried?
What has happened to the profits of Bloggs Ltd?
Is this good for business?

Make a sentence describing what the manager has done to his workers.
Think of another way of saying **lay off**.
Now turn to page 91 to check your answer.

put forward

Why is the man standing?
Who is he talking to?
What is he talking about?
What is the problem?

Does the man have an idea of how to solve the traffic problem?
What is his idea?
Make a sentence describing what he is doing in front of the planning committee now.
Think of another way of saying **put forward**.
Now turn to page 93 to check your answer.

Complete these sentences using the six verbs from this unit. Use each verb only once.

1 The United Nation's Peace Committee _____ a very interesting plan for achieving world peace.
2 There was a loud explosion as the terrorists _____ their threat to bomb the embassy.
3 The factory had to _____ many employees because of a drop in sales.
4 My boss _____ my request for a pay rise.
5 Jane's plan to move to a bigger flat _____ when she lost her job.
6 Paul _____ of university because he found the work too difficult.

Change these sentences into the passive. Do not include the agent in your answer.
EXAMPLE The company laid off ten employees.
        Ten employees were laid off.

1 A scientist is carrying out the tests now.
2 My boss laid me off.
3 The chairperson put forward a new proposal.
4 She turned down their application.

Replace the words in italics by the words in brackets. Change the word order if necessary.
EXAMPLE The doctor carried out *the tests*. (them)
        The doctor carried them out.

1 Henry turned *it* down. (the offer of a new job)
2 A soldier must carry out *orders*. (them)
3 Tom put forward *an interesting plan*. (it)
4 The company laid *them* off. (hundreds of manual workers)

Complete the passage using **carry out/fall through/lay off**.
Three months ago the company's plan to expand _____ and it had to _____ nearly half of its work force. The employees were very annoyed about this and they _____ their threat to go on strike.

Complete the passage using **turn down/drop out/put forward**.

Last week we had a committee meeting to organize a Christmas party in our office. I _____ some interesting suggestions but they were all _____, so I decided to _____ of the committee and let the others do all the work.

Use the verbs in brackets to reply to the following.
EXAMPLE Why are you looking so unhappy? (turn down)
POSSIBLE REPLY Because I asked my girlfriend to marry me, and she **turned** me **down**.

1 Did your scheme succeed? (fall through)
2 Why isn't Jim at work today? (lay off)
3 Why does the doctor want to take a sample of my blood. (carry out)
4 Did you take the money your father offered you? (turn down)
5 What happened at the meeting? (put forward)
6 Are you enjoying university? (drop out)

Unit 19

go off

What can you see in the picture?
What do you think is going to happen?

Make a sentence describing what the bomb has done.
Think of another way of saying **go off**.
Now turn to page 91 to check your answer.

put out

Is the light on?

Make a sentence describing what the man has done to the light.
Think of another way of saying **put out**.
Now turn to page 94 to check your answer.

blow up (1)

What do you think the man is going to do?

Make a sentence describing what the man has done to the house.
Think of another way of saying **blow up**.
Now turn to page 86 to check your answer.

cut down on

LAST YEAR

THIS YEAR

Did this man smoke a lot last year?
Do you think it was good for his health?
Why not?

Has he stopped smoking this year?
Is he smoking as much?
Does he look healthier?
Make a sentence describing what the man has done about smoking this year.
Think of another way of saying **cut down on**.
Now turn to page 88 to check your answer.

Unit 19

blow up (2)

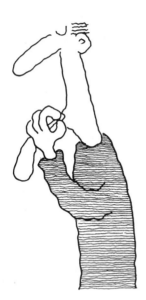

What is the man holding?

Make a sentence describing what the man is doing to the balloon.
Think of another way of saying **blow up**.
Now turn to page 86 to check your answer.

break out

What kind of vehicle can you see in the picture?
When are vehicles like this one used?
What is the vehicle doing now?
Why were tanks used between 1914–1918 and 1939–1945?
Make a sentence describing what happened in 1914 and again in 1939.
Think of another way of saying **break out**.
Now turn to page 86 to check your answer.

Complete these sentences using the six verbs from this unit. Use each verb only once.

1 My friend, Harry, was killed when the gun he was cleaning suddenly _____.
2 The soldiers _____ the enemy tank.
3 The Great Fire of London _____ in the year 1666.
4 Give me the pump and I'll _____ the tyres on your bicycle.
5 The firemen _____ the fire in the warehouse.
6 When I lost my job I had to _____ my spending.

Complete the sentences using the verbs in brackets.

1 (break out) A fight _____
2 (blow up) The soldiers put explosives on the bridge and _____
3 (go off) We lit the fireworks and _____
4 (blow up) Give me the bicycle pump and _____
5 (put out) If you don't want me to smoke I'll _____
6 (cut down on) You're too fat, you must _____

Replace the words in italics by the words in brackets. Change the word order if necessary.
EXAMPLE James put out *the fire*. (it)
       James put it out.

1 We blew *them* up. (as many balloons as we could find)
2 You must cut down on *the number of telephone calls you make*. (them)
3 The terrorists blew *it* up. (the aeroplane)
4 Please put *it* out. (your cigar)

Complete the passage using **cut down on/put out/blow up**.

Last Christmas I was driving home from a party when a policeman stopped my car. First, he asked me to _____ my cigarette; and then he told me to _____ a plastic bag that measured the amount of alcohol in my blood. After this he checked the bag and warned me that if I didn't _____ my drinking I would lose my driving licence.

Complete the passage using **go off/break out/blow up**.

Fighting _____ between rival gangs after the big football match. Shop windows were smashed and many alarms _____. One of the gangs even tried to _____ the supermarket with petrol bombs.

Use the verbs in brackets to reply to the following.
EXAMPLE That light is too bright. (put out)
POSSIBLE REPLY Don't worry, I'll **put** it **out**.

1 How was that bridge destroyed? (blow up)
2 What are you going to do about your weight? (cut down on)
3 Didn't you see that 'no smoking' sign? (put out)
4 Your car tyres are flat. (blow up)
5 What was that noise? (go off)
6 What happened in 1914*? (break out)
* World War 1 started in 1914.

Unit 20

get through (2)

What is the time?
Has he got a lot of work to do?

What is the time now?
Is there a lot of work to do now?
Make a sentence describing what he has done about the work.
Think of another way of saying **get through**.

Now turn to page 90 to check your answer.

hold up (2)

BANK

DEPOSITS

Do you think the man on the left is a customer?
Why do you think he is wearing a mask and holding a gun?
Make a sentence describing what he is doing.
Think of another way of saying **hold up**.

Now turn to page 91 to check your answer.

run out of

What is he thinking about?
Why do you think he is opening the bread-bin?
What do you think he is going to do?

Why do you think he looks disappointed?
Make a sentence describing what his problem is.
Think of another way of saying **run out of**.
Now turn to page 94 to check your answer.

break into

Do you think this is the man's house? Why not?
Why do you think he is wearing a mask and carrying a sack?
Make a sentence describing what the man is doing.
Think of another way of saying **break into**.
Now turn to page 86 to check your answer.

Unit 20

---

burn down

What is wrong with this house?

Is the house still on fire?
What condition is the house in?
Make a sentence describing what has happened to the house.
Think of another way of saying **burn down**.
Now turn to page 87 to check your answer.

---

wear out (2)

What is he doing?
Do you think the box is heavy? Why?
Do you think it is difficult for him to carry the box?

How does he look?
Make a sentence describing what carrying the box has done to him.
Think of another way of saying **wear out**.
Now turn to page 96 to check your answer.

Complete these sentences using the six verbs from this unit. Use each verb only once.

1 I must go to the bank because I've _____ cash.
2 A gang of terrorists _____ the embassy with a petrol bomb.
3 It was such a good book that I _____ it in one evening.
4 Decorating the house all day has _____ me _____.
5 My younger brother _____ my money box and stole my savings.
6 Bandits _____ the bus and robbed the passengers.

Change these sentences into the passive.
EXAMPLE A mugger held me up.
        I was held up by a mugger.

1 A burglar broke into my flat.
2 Cleaning the house wore him out.
3 Some men held up the van.
4 Some terrorists burned down the embassy.

Replace the words in italics by the words in brackets. Change the word order if necessary.
EXAMPLE The robbers held up *the train*. (it)
        The robbers held it up.

1 Looking after the children wore *them* out. (the nurses in the hospital)
2 Three men held *it* up. (my uncle's newspaper shop)
3 Someone broke into *our house*. (it)
4 John got through *his homework*. (it)
5 They burned *it* down. (part of the city)

Complete the passage using **run out of/wear out/burn down**.

My father is a fireman. Yesterday he helped fight a big fire in a warehouse. When he got home he was _____. Unfortunately, the warehouse _____ because the firemen _____ water.

Complete the passage using **get through/hold up/break into**.

I was working at the bank trying to _____ the weekly accounts when some gunmen _____ my office and _____ me _____.

Use the verbs in brackets to reply to the following.
EXAMPLE Could I have a cold drink? (run out of)
POSSIBLE REPLY No, I'm sorry you can't because I've **run out of** ice.

1 Would you like to go dancing tonight? (wear out)
2 What happened to the old cinema? (burn down)
3 Why were you in such a hurry this morning? (run out of)
4 How did you get all this money? (hold up)
5 Why did you come home from work so early? (get through)
6 Why did the police arrest you? (break into)

Reference Section

be off (1)   *usually used in the present tense*

(of an event / an arrangement etc.) to be cancelled.

The lead singer of 'The Rolling Beatles' pop group is ill, so tonight's concert **is off**.

> The concert **is off**.

be off (2)

(of food) to have gone bad.

Nick decided to have a fried egg for breakfast, but there was a terrible smell when he cracked the egg. 'This egg **is off**,' he thought. 'I can't eat it.'

> The egg **is off**.

be over

to be finished.

The storm **is over**; it has stopped raining and the sun is shining.

> The storm **is over**.

be taken aback   *used in the passive*

to be surprised and confused.

Jeff **was taken aback** when he opened the door and discovered an elephant.

> Jeff **was taken aback** by the discovery of an elephant.
> Jeff **was taken aback**.

beat up

to hurt someone badly by hitting and punching.

Two men **beat** Fred **up** and left him lying unconscious on the pavement.

> They **beat up** Fred.
> They **beat** Fred **up**.
> They **beat** him **up**.

blow up (1)

to destroy (something or someone) by explosion; to explode.

Mr Trent hated his house, so he **blew** it **up** with dynamite and built a new one instead.

> Mr Trent **blew up** his house.
> Mr Trent **blew** his house **up**.
> Mr Trent **blew** it **up**.
> The house **blew up**.

blow up (2)   a balloon / a tyre / a football etc.

to fill with air; to inflate.

Uncle Joe **blew up** the balloons for the Christmas party.

> Uncle Joe **blew up** the balloons.
> Uncle Joe **blew** the balloons **up**.
> Uncle Joe **blew** them **up**.

break down (1)

(of machinery) to stop working.

Tom's car **broke down** on the way to the airport, and he had to get a taxi.

> His car **broke down**.

break down (2)

to lose control emotionally or mentally.

Alec **broke down** and cried when his mother died.

> Alec **broke down**.

break into   a building / a bank / a house etc.

to enter somewhere (e.g. a house) illegally, especially by force.

Last night a burglar **broke into** my house and stole my television set.

> A burglar **broke into** my house.
> A burglar **broke into** it.

break off   talks / negotiations / an engagement / a relationship / an agreement etc.

to end; to interrupt; to discontinue.

Peace talks between the U.S.S.R. and the U.S.A. have **broken off** after three days of serious disagreement.

> Peace talks between the U.S.S.R. and the U.S.A. have **broken off**.
> The U.S.A. has **broken off** peace talks with the U.S.S.R.
> They have **broken off** peace talks.
> They have **broken** them **off**.

break out

(of unpleasant things e.g. wars, epidemics, fires, violence etc.) to start, usually suddenly.

The Second World War **broke out** on 3 September, 1939.

> In 1939 World War Two **broke out**.
> World War Two **broke out** in 1939.
> World War Two **broke out** on 3 September, 1939.

break out in spots / a rash / a cold sweat*

to become covered by (something).

Cyril **broke out** in spots this morning.

> He **broke out in** spots.
> He **broke out in** them.

to show signs of great fear.

break up (1)

(of a marriage / a family / a relationship etc.) to end; to separate.

The Greens' marriage **broke up** in 1985 after only two years.

> Their marriage **broke up**.
> They **broke up**.
> Money trouble **broke up** their marriage.
> Money trouble **broke** it **up**.

break up (2) an activity

to stop.

The headmaster **broke up** the fight between Roger and Clive.

> The headmaster **broke up** the fight.
> The headmaster **broke** the fight **up**.
> The headmaster **broke** it **up**.
> The fight **broke up**.

bring up

to take care of a child until it is fully grown and able to care for itself; to train and prepare a child for adult life.

Joe's mother **brought** him **up** well. She loved him, cared for him and taught him how to behave himself. Now he is a polite young man and his mother is proud of him.

> She **brought up** Joe.
> She **brought** Joe **up**.
> She **brought** him **up**.

Note: Children are educated at school.

brush up

to improve your knowledge, skill, or memory of (something you used to know, or do, but have now partly forgotten).

Frank's visit to the international business conference in Paris was a disaster because his French was so bad. His boss said, 'When you get back to England you must **brush up** your French by enrolling in an evening class.'

> Frank must **brush up** his French.
> Frank must **brush** his French **up**.
> Frank must **brush** it **up**.

burn down

(usually of buildings) to destroy by burning.

My house **burned down** last night. In the morning it was just a pile of ashes.

> My house **burned down**.
> Someone **burned down** my house.
> Someone **burned** my house **down**.
> Someone **burned** it **down**.

call off an event / an arrangement / an activity etc. *often used in the passive*

to cancel something; to abandon something that has already begun.

The Football Association **called off** the match between England and Greece because of bad weather.

> The Football Association **called off** the match.
> The Football Association **called** the match **off**.
> The Football Association **called** it **off**.
> The match was **called off**. (*passive*)

calm down a person / a difficult situation etc.

to become less excited and tense; to help someone (or a difficult situation) to become less excited and tense.

My father was very angry and it took him ten minutes to **calm down**.

> My father **calmed down**.
> We **calmed down** my father.
> We **calmed** my father **down**.
> We **calmed** him **down**.

carry out instructions / a duty / an order / a threat / a test etc.

to fulfill or perform (something).

Sergeant Jones ordered Private Wilson to push the waggon across the field. The waggon was very heavy but Private Wilson **carried out** his orders without complaining.

> He **carried out** his orders.
> He **carried** his orders **out**.
> He **carried** them **out**.

catch on

to become popular.

David's strange new hair-style is really **catching on**; all the young boys in the neighbourhood are copying it.

> David's new hair-style is **catching on**.

Reference Section

check in   at a hotel, an airport etc.

to report one's arrival.

Jack took a taxi to the hotel and **checked in**.

> Jack **checked in**.
> Jack **checked in** at the hotel.
> Jack **checked in** to the hotel.

Note: When Jack left the hotel he checked out.

cheer up

to become happier.

Jack was feeling unhappy, but he **cheered up** when he heard that he had passed his exam.

> Jack **cheered up**.
> The good news **cheered** Jack **up**.
> The good news **cheered up** Jack.
> The good news **cheered** him **up**.

come across   something or someone

to find or meet by chance.

A lucky tramp **came across** a wallet full of money as he was walking down the street.

> He **came across** a wallet.
> He **came across** it.

come into   money/property/a fortune etc.

to receive something (usually money or property) after someone's death.

Peter **came into** a fortune when his father died.

> Peter **came into** a fortune.
> Peter **came into** it.

come round or **come to**

to regain consciousness.

James fainted when the air-conditioning stopped working. Two of his colleagues took care of him until he **came round** (**came to**).

> James **came round**.
> James **came to**.

come up with   an idea / a plan / a suggestion etc.

to think of; to produce.

Arnold and his girlfriend were separated by a deep ravine. Eventually, Arnold **came up with** the idea of cutting down a tree and using it as a bridge.

> He **came up with** the idea.
> He **came up with** it.

cut down on   smoking / cigarettes / drinking / spending / production etc.

to reduce in size or amount.

Last year Peter was very ill and his doctor told him to **cut down on** the number of cigarettes he smoked. This year Peter smokes much less and feels a lot better.

> Peter **cut down on** cigarettes.
> Peter **cut down on** them.
> Peter **cut down on** smoking.

cut off   *often used in the passive*

This verb can refer to either:

a) the service or supply that is cut off e.g. water, electricity, etc. or
b) the person who is cut off.

to disconnect, interrupt or discontinue something or someone.

Paul was talking to Anna on the telephone. Suddenly they couldn't hear each other. Paul phoned Anna again immediately. 'What happened?' Anna asked him. 'We were **cut off**,' replied Paul.

> The operator **cut** them **off**.
> The operator **cut off** their call.
> They were **cut off**. (*passive*)

die out

to disappear completely; to become extinct.

The great dinosaurs **died out** millions of years ago.

> The dinosaurs **died out**.

do up (1)   a house / a room / a flat / an old car etc.

to repair; to improve the condition and appearance of something.

When Bob and Sally bought their house it was in a bad state, so they spent six months **doing** it **up**. The house looked beautiful by the time they finished.

> They **did** the house **up**.
> They **did up** the house.
> They **did** it **up**.

do up (2)   a shoelace / a zip / a dress / a coat etc.

to fasten; to button; to zip; to tie.

It was a very cold day, so Brian **did up** all the buttons on his overcoat.

> He **did up** the buttons.
> He **did** the buttons **up**.
> He **did** them **up**.

drop in

to pay a short visit, often without warning.

Laura was shopping near her friend, Lynn, and decided to **drop in** and see her.

> Laura **dropped in** to see Lynn.
> Laura **dropped in** to see her.
> Laura **dropped in** on Lynn.
> Laura **dropped in** on her.
> Laura **dropped in**.

drop off (1) something or someone

to stop a vehicle and let someone get out; to take something (or someone) to a place and leave it there.

David drove his wife, Sue, into town and **dropped** her **off** at the cinema.

> David **dropped off** his wife.
> David **dropped** his wife **off**.
> David **dropped** her **off**.

drop off (2)

to fall asleep (often unintentionally).

John sat in his favourite armchair and **dropped off**. Five minutes later, his young son came into the room and woke him.

> He **dropped off**.

drop out

to withdraw from, or stop taking part in (a competition, a social group, a school, a university, a job etc.).

Sam **dropped out** of the race because he felt tired and ill.

> He **dropped out** of the race.
> He **dropped out**.

fall out

to quarrel.

George and Sam went out for dinner together. The evening ended badly because they **fell out** over who should pay the bill.

> George **fell out** with* Sam over** the bill.
> George and Sam **fell out**.

* fall out with a person
** fall out over something

fall through

to fail to happen or be completed (of plans, arrangements, schemes etc.).

Eric's plan to go on a skiing holiday **fell through** because he broke his leg.

> His plan **fell through**.

fill in a form / a questionnaire etc.

to complete (a form).

It took me an hour to **fill in** the application form.

> It took me an hour to **fill in** the form.
> It took me an hour to **fill** the form **in**.
> It took me an hour to **fill** it **in**.

find out the truth / a secret / an address / the time / when / what / why / where / who / which etc.

to make an effort to discover or get to know (something).

Mr Jones wanted to catch the train to London. He was late and he didn't know which platform the London train left from. He **found out** which platform by asking a ticket collector.

> He **found out** which platform the train left from.
> He didn't know which platform the train left from so he **found out**.
> He didn't know the number of the platform so he **found** it **out**.

get away

to escape.

The prisoner **got away** from his guards and ran into the forest.

> The prisoner **got away** from his guards.
> The prisoner **got away** from them.
> The prisoner **got away**.

get away with

to do something wrong or illegal without being punished (usually without even being discovered or caught).

Last year Jack robbed a bank and **got away with** it; the police didn't even find his fingerprints. Nowadays Jack lives a life of luxury on a beautiful tropical island.

> Jack **got away with** the bank robbery.
> Jack **got away with** robbing the bank.
> Jack **got away with** it.

get over an illness / a failure / a difficulty / a shock etc.

to recover from (something).

Sam has **got over** his operation and expects to leave hospital tomorrow.

> He has **got over** his operation.
> He has **got over** it.

Reference Section

get round (1) a problem / a difficulty etc.

to solve or avoid a problem.

Brian and Dan couldn't move the wardrobe because it was too heavy. They **got round** the problem by putting the wardrobe on a trolley and pushing it.

> They **got round** the problem.
> They **got round** it.

get round (2) someone

to persuade someone to do what you want; to persuade someone to let you do what you want.

Tim wanted some sweets, but his father told him they were bad for his teeth. After five minutes of persuasion, Tim managed to **get round** his father and they both went into the sweet shop.

> Tim **got round** his father.
> Tim **got round** him.

get through (1)

to contact someone (usually by telephone).

Jim (phoning his friend Roger): Hello, Roger. I've been trying to **get through** to you for hours!
Roger: Sorry, Jim. I had to make a lot of calls this morning.

> Jim tried to **get through** to Roger.
> Jim tried to **get through** to him.
> Jim tried to **get through**.

get through (2) some work / a task / a book etc.

to finish; to complete.

Roger had a lot of work to do yesterday, but he **got through** it all by five o'clock.

> Roger **got through** his work.
> Roger **got through** it.

give in

to stop resisting; to surrender.

The fight between Tom and Dick stopped when Tom hurt his hand and had to **give in**.

> Tom **gave in**.

give out books / examination papers / pills etc.

to give (something or things) to each person in a group of people; to distribute.

The teacher **gave out** the books, so that the pupils could read the story.

> The teacher **gave out** the books.
> The teacher **gave** the books **out**.
> The teacher **gave** them **out**.

give (oneself) up (1)

to surrender oneself (usually to someone).

The police surrounded the criminal's house and ordered him to **give** himself **up**. After a few minutes, he came out and they took him to the police station.

> The criminal **gave** himself **up** to the police.
> The criminal **gave** himself **up**.

give up (2)

to stop trying to do something (often because it is too difficult).

One day a hungry dog saw a bunch of juicy grapes hanging from a vine. The dog tried very hard to get the grapes, but it couldn't jump high enough to reach them. After ten frustrating minutes, the dog **gave up** the attempt and walked home angrily.

> The dog **gave up** the attempt.
> The dog **gave** the attempt **up**.
> The dog **gave** it **up**.
> The dog **gave up** trying to get the grapes.
> The dog **gave up** trying.
> The dog **gave up**.

give up (3)

(of an habitual activity, smoking / drinking / a job etc.) to stop doing or having (something).

Howard decided to **give up** cigarettes after seeing a poster on the dangers of smoking.

> Howard **gave up** cigarettes.
> Howard **gave** cigarettes **up**.
> Howard **gave** them **up**.
> Howard **gave up** smoking.

go down

to become less swollen.

Phil's cheek became swollen because he had a bad toothache. The dentist treated his bad tooth and his swollen cheek soon **went down**.

> His swollen cheek **went down**.

go for a person, an animal.

to attack.

The dog **went for** Joe and hurt his arm.

> The dog **went for** Joe.
> The dog **went for** him.

Note: this verb is not used in the passive.

go off

(of explosive devices e.g. bombs, guns etc.) to explode or fire; (of alarms or alarm clocks) to ring suddenly.

Many people were killed when the bomb **went off**.

The bomb **went off**.
---

go through

to examine (something).

When Ben entered this country, a custom's officer **went through** his suitcase. The officer took all of Ben's clothes out of his suitcase and looked at them very carefully.

A custom's officer **went through** Ben's suitcase.
A custom's officer **went through** it.
---

go with

to match or suit (something).

Tom wanted to see if checked trousers **go with** a striped jacket; he looked in a mirror and thought they looked horrible together. After trying a few other pairs of trousers he decided that striped trousers **go with** a striped jacket.

Striped trousers **go with** a striped jacket.
Striped trousers **go with** it.
---

grow up

to develop from a child into an adult.

Joe has **grown up** into a fine young man.

Joe has **grown up**.
---

hold on

to wait (especially on the telephone).

George phoned his office because he wanted some information. '**Hold on** a minute and I'll get it for you,' said his assistant.

His assistant asked him to **hold on**.
---

hold up (1)   *usually used in the passive*

to stop; to delay.

The traffic was **held up** for a few hours because of an accident that blocked the road.

The accident **held up** the traffic.
The accident **held** the traffic **up**.
The accident **held** it **up**.
The traffic was **held up**. (*passive*)
---

hold up (2)   a person / a bank / a vehicle etc.

to rob, especially using a weapon (e.g. a gun).

Earlier today a masked robber with a gun **held up** the bank and escaped with a hundred thousand pounds.

A robber **held up** the bank.
A robber **held** the bank **up**.
A robber **held** it **up**.
---

lay off   *often passive*

to stop employing (a worker), often for a short time because there is not enough work.

Last year the manager of Bloggs Ltd **laid off** a hundred workers because business was very bad.

He **laid off** a hundred workers.
He **laid** a hundred workers **off**.
He **laid** them **off**.
They were **laid off**. (*passive*)
---

let down

to disappoint someone (often by breaking a promise or an agreement).

Julia promised to meet Rick outside the cinema at eight o'clock, but she **let** him **down**. He waited for two hours and then he went home angrily.

Julia **let** Rick **down**.
Julia **let** him **down**.
---

let off

to excuse (someone) from (a punishment, a duty, or doing something).

Bill should have been sent to prison for six months, but the judge decided to **let** him **off** so that he could stay out of prison and take care of his family.

The judge **let** Bill **off** going to prison.
The judge **let** him **off** the punishment.
The judge **let** Bill **off**.
---

let out

to allow (a person or an animal) to leave (a place); to release.

They **let** Fred **out** of prison after five years.

They **let** Fred **out** of prison.
They **let** Fred **out**.
They **let** him **out**.
---

look after   someone or something

to take care of someone or something.

Looking after a baby is a full-time job. You have to bath it, dress it and feed it.

She **looks after** the baby.
She **looks after** it.

Reference Section

look back

to remember and think about the past.

The Blacks have been married for many years. They like talking about the past and **looking back** on old times. At the moment they are looking at pictures of their wedding.

They enjoy **looking back**	on at to	old times.

They enjoy **looking back** on them.
They enjoy **looking back**.

look down on someone or something

to think that someone (or something) is inferior, low or worthless; to disapprove of (someone or something).

Sir Douglas is a very rich aristocrat. Fred is a very poor tramp. Sir Douglas thinks that he is a much better person than Fred – he **looks down on** Fred.

Sir Douglas **looks down on** Fred.
Sir Douglas **looks down on** him.

look for something or someone

to try to find (something or someone), often a thing or person that is lost.

Fred wanted to open his front door but he couldn't find his key. He **looked for** it everywhere. 'It's in one of my pockets,' he thought.

He **looked for** his key.
He **looked for** it.

look forward to a future event

to think with pleasure about a future event that you expect to enjoy.

Bill Bloggs has been in prison for the last ten years. Next year he'll be released from prison and he'll be a free man. Bill is **looking forward to** next year.

Bill is **looking forward to** next year.
Bill is **looking forward to** it.
Bill is **looking forward to** leaving prison.

look into a situation / a crime / a problem / a complaint etc.

to investigate; to carefully examine a situation or event and try to discover the reasons for it.

The police are **looking into** the death of Mr James. They want to know how he was murdered. They are looking at the evidence and asking lots of questions. They want to find the murderer.

The police are **looking into** the murder of Mr James.
The police are **looking into** it.

look over some work / a car / a house / a document / a suggestion / an applicant etc.

to examine (someone or something) carefully and fully.

Joe wanted to buy a second-hand car. 'That one looks good,' he said to the salesman. 'Give me some time to **look** it **over**. If it's in good condition, I'll buy it.'

He **looked** the car **over**.
He **looked over** the car.
He **looked** it **over**.

look round a house / a shop / a town / a factory / an exhibition etc.

to visit and tour round a place.

Mr and Mrs Smith wanted to buy a house. The estate agent took them to see a house in the centre of town and said, '**Look round** the house and see if it's what you want.'

They **looked round** the house.
They **looked round** it.
They went into the house and **looked round**.

look up a word / a telephone number / an address / a train time / a date etc.

to find (or try to find) something (e.g. a telephone number) in a book (e.g. a telephone directory).

While Peter was reading he found a word that he didn't understand. 'This is a difficult word,' he thought. 'I'll **look** it **up** in the dictionary and see what it means.'

He **looked up** the word.
He **looked** the word **up**.
He **looked** it **up**.

look up to someone

to respect (someone); to admire (someone).

Young Jimmy's favourite footballer is Ted Ross of Arsenal. Jimmy **looks up to** Ted and he tries to be like him.

Jimmy **looks up to** Ted Ross.
Jimmy **looks up to** him.

make out (1)   *often used in the negative with can't and couldn't*

to see, hear, or understand (something or someone), often with difficulty.

Bob saw something on the horizon as he was looking through his binoculars. At first he couldn't **make out** what it was, but after a few minutes he could just **make out** the shape of a yacht.

He couldn't **make out** the thing on the horizon.
He couldn't **make** the thing **out**.
He couldn't **make** it **out**.

make out (2) a cheque

to write (a cheque).

I **made out** a cheque for ten pounds.

> I **made out** a cheque.
> I **made** a cheque **out**.
> I **made** it **out**.

make up (1)

to become friends again after a quarrel.

Yesterday Joan and Jack had a big argument about politics. Earlier today they decided to forget their differences and **make up**.

> Joan and Jack **made up**.
> Joan and Jack **made up** their quarrel.
> Joan and Jack **made** it **up**.
> Jack **made up** with Joan.
> Jack **made it up** with Joan.
> Jack **made** (it) **up** with her.

make up (2) a story / a poem / an excuse / an explanation etc.

to invent, sometimes with the purpose of deception.

Colin overslept and was late for work. It was the third time he had overslept that month, so he decided to **make up** an excuse. He told his boss that the engine of his car had exploded.

> He **made up** an excuse.
> He **made** an excuse **up**.
> He **made** it **up**.

make up for a mistake / doing or not doing something etc.

to compensate for.

June and Ron arranged to meet outside the cinema at 7.30 p.m. June was very upset when Ron arrived an hour late. Ron **made up for** being late by apologizing to June and giving her a big bunch of flowers.

> He **made up for** being late.
> He **made up for** it.

Note: the object is very often it.

mistake for

to think wrongly that (one thing or person) is (another thing or person).

I frightened myself last night when I **mistook** a piece of old rope **for** a dangerous snake.

> I **mistook** a piece of old rope **for** a dangerous snake.
> I saw a piece of old rope and I **mistook** it **for** a dangerous snake.

own up

to tell (someone) that you have done something wrong, or that you are at fault.

James **owned up** to drawing a silly picture of his teacher on the board.

> He **owned up** to drawing the picture.
> He **owned up** to the naughty trick.
> He **owned up**.

pass away   pass on   pass over

(usually of a person) to die.

Fred Bloggs **passed away (passed on/passed over)** in 1985 after a long illness.

> Fred **passed away**.
> Fred **passed on**.
> Fred **passed over**.

pass out

to lose consciousness.

When the air-conditioning stopped working, James found it difficult to breathe and **passed out**.

> He **passed out**.

pick up something or someone

to give someone a ride in a vehicle; to collect someone or something (sometimes in a vehicle).

Jeff was driving home when he saw a hitchhiker. He stopped the car and **picked** the hitchhiker **up**.

> Jeff **picked up** the hitchhiker.
> Jeff **picked** the hitchhiker **up**.
> Jeff **picked** him **up**.

point out something or someone

to draw attention to something or someone.

My uncle showed me the building he used to work in and he **pointed out** his old office on the sixth floor.

> He **pointed out** his office.
> He **pointed** his office **out**.
> He **pointed** it **out**.

put forward a proposal / a plan / a suggestion / an idea etc.

to offer (a proposal / a plan etc.) for consideration.

Mr Smith **put forward** the idea of introducing traffic lights at the crossroads as a way of preventing traffic jams. The planning committee thought his idea was very good.

> He **put forward** the idea.
> He **put** the idea **forward**.
> He **put** it **forward**.

Reference Section

put off (1)   an event / doing something etc.

to delay doing something until a later date; to delay an event or arrangement until a later date.

Martin was very unhappy when he saw the huge pile of dirty dishes in the kitchen. He felt a little happier after deciding to **put off** the washing-up until the next day.

> Martin **put off** the washing-up until the next day.
> Martin **put** the washing-up **off** till the next day.
> Martin **put** it **off** until the next day.
> Martin **put off** do**ing** the washing-up till the next day.
> Martin **put off** wash**ing** up until the next day.

put (someone) off (2)

to discourage, or distract, (someone) from doing something.

Ron was trying to read, but the noise from the television **put** him **off** and he had to stop.

> The noise from the T.V. **put** Ron **off** his book.
> The noise from the T.V. **put** him **off** his book.
> The noise from the T.V. **put** Ron **off** read**ing** his book.
> The noise from the T.V. **put** him **off**.

put on   clothes / glasses / a ring / a necklace etc.

to dress oneself.

Perry **put on** his new sweater because he wanted to wear it for work.

> Perry **put on** his sweater.
> Perry **put** his sweater **on**.
> Perry **put** it **on**.

put out   a cigarette / a light / a fire etc.

to extinguish.

Steve **put out** the light in the lounge before going upstairs to bed.

> Steve **put out** the light.
> Steve **put** the light **out**.
> Steve **put** it **out**.

put through

to connect a telephone caller to the number he or she wants.

Mr Pratt phoned the offices of Gunn and Company. 'Who would you like to speak to?' asked the switchboard operator. '**Put** me **through** to Mr Gunn please,' Mr Pratt replied.

> She **put** Mr Pratt **through** to Mr Gunn.
> She **put** him **through** to Mr Gunn.
> She **put through** Mr Pratt's call.

put up with

to suffer (a difficult situation or person) without complaining.

When Uncle Mike comes to visit us, the children behave very badly. They hit him, they play tricks on him and they make a lot of noise. Uncle Mike must love them very much because he **puts up with** everything they do, and he never gets annoyed with them.

> Uncle Mike **puts up with** their bad behaviour.
> Uncle Mike **puts up with** it.

run in   a motor cycle / a new car / a machine etc.

to use a new (or reconditioned) engine carefully until it is ready for normal use.

George is **running in** his new car, so he can't drive fast.

> George is **running in** his new car.
> George is **running** it **in**.
> **Running in**, please pass. (*a notice sometimes seen on new cars*)

run into   someone

to meet by chance.

I was on my way to work when I **ran into** Jeremy Thomas. It was a lovely surprise because I hadn't seen him for a long time.

> I **ran into** Jeremy.
> I **ran into** him.
> We **ran into** each other.

run out of   coffee / sugar / money / patience / time etc.

to use all of (something) and have no more left.

Howard has **run out of** bread, so he can't make himself a sandwich. If he wants a sandwich, he'll have to go to the baker's shop and buy some more bread.

> Howard has **run out of** bread.
> Howard has **run out of** it.

see off

to say goodbye to someone who is going on a journey at the place (e.g. airport, station etc.) where the journey begins.

Bill arranged to go to Scotland to stay with his grandmother for a few days. His father, Frank, drove him to the railway station and **saw** him **off**.

> Frank **saw** Bill **off**.
> Frank **saw** him **off**.

set off

to start a journey.

Barry **set off** on his camping holiday at six o'clock in the morning and reached the campsite, in France, at midday.

> Barry **set off**.
> Barry **set off** at six o'clock.
> Barry **set off** on a camping holiday.
> Barry **set off** for France.

soak up a liquid / information / knowledge / punishment etc.

to absorb; to become filled with (something).

The sponge **soaked up** the spilt milk.

> The sponge **soaked up** the milk.
> The sponge **soaked** the milk **up**.
> The sponge **soaked** it **up**.

speak up *often used in the imperative*

to speak louder.

Terry was talking to his grandfather. '**Speak up**, Terry,' his grandfather said. 'I'm a bit deaf and I can't hear you.'

> Grandfather told Terry to **speak up**.
> Grandfather said, '**Speak up**'.

stand for

to represent or mean; to be a sign or short form of something else.

The letters B.B.C. **stand for** the British Broadcasting Corporation.

> B.B.C. **stands for** British Broadcasting Corporation.
> What do the letters B.B.C. **stand for**?

take after someone

to look or be like an older relative.

Little Christopher **takes after** his father. He has black hair, big feet and a bad temper just like his dad.

> Christopher **takes after** his father.
> Christopher **takes after** him.

take down a statement / a telephone number / some information etc.

to record in writing.

When the policeman arrived at the scene of the accident he **took down** the witness's statement.

> He **took down** the statement.
> He **took** the statement **down**.
> He **took** it **down**.

take in *often used in the passive*

to deceive (someone); to cheat (someone).

The hungry wolf had a problem: all the sheep in the neighbourhood knew him and ran away when they saw him. After some thought he decided to disguise himself as a sheep. The neighbourhood sheep were **taken in** by the wolf's clever disguise and he was able to walk up to them and catch one of them for his dinner.

> The sheep were **taken in** by the wolf's disguise. (*passive*)
> The wolf's disguise **took in** the sheep.
> The wolf's disguise **took** the sheep **in**.
> The wolf's disguise **took** them **in**.

take off (1)

(of an aeroplane) to rise from the ground.

At the beginning of a journey an aeroplane **takes off**. At the end of a journey an aeroplane lands.

> The aeroplane **took off**.

take off (2)

to remove anything that is worn on the body (especially clothes).

Nick **took off** his jacket because he was feeling very hot.

> Nick **took off** his jacket.
> Nick **took** his jacket **off**.
> Nick **took** it **off**.

take over

to assume responsibility for, or control of, (something or a situation) from someone else.

Simon **took over** the manager's job from Mr Jones when he retired.

> Simon **took over** the manager's job from Mr Jones.
> Simon **took over** the manager's job.
> Simon **took** the manager's job **over**.
> Simon **took** it **over**.
> Simon **took over**.

take up a hobby / a sport / a job / a habit etc.

to begin to study, practise, or do (something).

Tim wanted to **take up** painting, so he joined an evening class at the local College of Art.

> He **took up** paint**ing**.
> He **took** paint**ing up**.
> He **took** it **up**.
> He **took up** a new hobby.

Reference Section

tear up a piece of paper / a letter / a newspaper etc.

to destroy completely by tearing.

Brian **tore up** the letter angrily.

> Brian **tore up** the letter.
> Brian **tore** the letter **up**.
> Brian **tore** it **up**.

tell off

to speak angrily to someone who has done something wrong; to find fault with someone.

Howard **told** his son **off** for breaking a window with his football.

> Howard **told off** his son.
> Howard **told** his son **off**.
> Howard **told** him **off**.
> Howard **told** him **off** for break**ing** a window.

think over a problem / a proposal / a situation etc.

to consider (something) carefully.

Owen is playing chess with a friend. At the moment he is **thinking over** his next move.

> He is **thinking over** his next move.
> He is **thinking** his next move **over**.
> He is **thinking** it **over**.

try on a hat / a new pair of shoes / a dress etc.

to put on an article of clothing to see if it fits and how it looks.

Last week I went into a shop and **tried on** three hats. The first hat was too big; the second one was too small; but the third one fitted me perfectly and looked good, so I bought it.

> I **tried on** three hats.
> I **tried** three hats **on**.
> I **tried** them **on**.

try out something or someone

to test something (or someone) by using it.

Angela saw an advertisement for a new soap powder called 'Zap'. She decided to **try** it **out** because she wanted to see if it was better than her usual soap powder.

> Angela **tried out** new 'Zap'.
> Angela **tried** new 'Zap' **out**.
> Angela **tried** it **out**.

turn down a request / an offer / an applicant / an application etc.

to refuse or reject (something or someone).

Jeff was interviewed for the job at Bloggs Ltd but they **turned** him **down** because he was too young.

> They **turned down** Jeff.
> They **turned** Jeff **down**.
> They **turned** him **down**.

turn into something or someone

to change; to become.

The beautiful princess kissed the frog and it **turned into** a handsome prince.

> The frog **turned into** a prince.
> The kiss **turned** the frog **into** a prince.

wear off

to disappear gradually.

The pain in Jim's foot **wore off** after he took some painkiller.

> The pain **wore off**.

wear out (1)

to use (something) until it becomes unfit for further use; to become unusable after excessive use.

Paul **wore out** his favourite jumper after wearing it every day for ten years.

> Paul **wore out** his jumper.
> Paul **wore** his jumper **out**.
> Paul **wore** it **out**.
> The jumper **wore out**.

wear out (2) *often used in the passive*

to tire greatly; to exhaust.

Carrying the heavy box across the street **wore** Fred **out**. When he got home he went straight to bed.

> Carrying the heavy box **wore out** Fred.
> Carrying the heavy box **wore** Fred **out**.
> Carrying the heavy box **wore** him **out**.
> Fred was **worn out** by carrying the heavy box.
> (*passive*)

work out a sum / a problem / a plan / a method etc.

to solve a problem by calculation or study; to produce a way of dealing with a problem or situation by thinking.

Jimmy is busy doing his homework. At the moment he is **working out** the answer to a sum.

> He is **working out** the answer.
> He is **working** the answer **out**.
> He is **working** it **out**.